Working Out With Weights

Steve Jarrell

PRENTICE
HALL
PRESS

New York   London   Toronto   Sydney   Tokyo   Singapore

Prentice Hall Press
15 Columbus Circle
New York, New York 10012

Published in 1988 by Prentice Hall Press
A Division of Simon & Schuster Inc.
Originally published by Arco Publishing, Inc.

PRENTICE HALL PRESS and colophons are registered
trademarks of Simon & Schuster Inc.

ISBN 0-668-04221-4

Manufactured in the United States of America

20   19   18   17   16   15   14   13

Contents

Introduction

The roots of this book go back to the winter of 1965–66, when I began weight training in the hope of bettering my performance as a sprinter and shot-putter on my high school track team. I felt so positive about my gains in strength and muscularity, I continued into competitive weightlifting. In 1971, a serious knee injury ended my career as a possible contender in Olympic lifting and powerlifting. Since then, I have been active as an official for both weightlifting and physique contests while still training hard on a non-competitive basis.

Just as valuable as my exchange of ideas with other competitive lifters over the years were my four years of weight training with both athletes and non-athletes at Middle Tennessee State University. We constantly tried new exercises and new programs in order to build maximum strength and size or aid in playing a sport.

When I began teaching in the fall of 1970, I also began to get requests from students for weight training information. I gave them basic advice concerning the exercises, diet, and amount of rest they needed. In turn, I asked that they keep me informed on the results of their training programs. This book is the culmination of those six years of work almost exclusively with junior high and high school students.

Working Out With Weights should answer the questions most junior high and high school students ask about weight training, weightlifting, and bodybuilding. It is intended to bridge the gap between the tersely worded manuals that come with barbell sets and the jumble of self-serving information appearing in some bodybuilding publications.

High school and junior high students demonstrate the exercises recommended in this book. The pictures show the actual results to be expected from weight training during the teens, not adults with years of advanced weight training.

There are several people to thank for putting this book together. Bill Johnson, owner of the Corinthian Spa in Tullahoma, Tennessee, and his staff graciously allowed the use of their facilities for much of the photography.

Robert Pierson Smith of Tullahoma took time out from his regular job as a motion picture producer to do most of the photography. Bob's pictures add visual impact to the book. Other photographic help came from Carl Scarbrough who took some pictures and developed most of the pictures for the book.

Thanks go to several Chattanooga, Tennessee, area high school and junior high school students, but especially to David Salstrand and Carl Betsch for demonstrating the exercises. Carl also held down the job of student coordinator, reading and rereading the manuscript, examining pictures, and giving some excellent advice along the way.

My greatest support came from Brenda Chauncey, my typist, proofreader, and good friend. She gets my biggest thanks.

Introducing our three main exercise demonstrators:
Ronnie Voss (left), Carl Betsch (right), and David Salstrand (seated).

Personal Observations

Over the past several years I have accumulated a great deal of weight training information pertaining to high school and junior high students. This information and subsequent insight was gained in several ways. Grateful students promptly and regularly reported gains in strength and size. Measurements were taken of muscles and maximum lifts, and multiple lifts were attempted to determine strength increases.

The ages of these students ranged from twelve to nineteen. Some were rather uncoordinated, poorly muscled, non-athletes. Others were state champions, superbly built and conditioned. In height, the students ranged from under five feet to six feet seven inches, and in weight from under 100 to over 200 pounds. Some were slightly below average in intelligence, while others recorded genius level brilliance.

Here are some brief conclusions drawn from these experiences:

- After puberty, the muscle tissue of a boy responds to progressive resistance training in the same manner as an adult.

- A junior high student is more likely to overtrain than undertrain; then lose interest.

- There is no stereotype for the student who wishes to use weights to improve himself.

- Students who disciplined themselves best to regular weight training tended to be more intelligent than those who worked out erratically.

- No student who used one of the author's programs and trained three times a week ever failed to gain in strength and physical size. Some of the gains, especially for junior high students, were remarkable.

- The chest, upper arms, and thighs appear to grow faster than other muscle groups.

- The bench press, behind the neck press, and curl, performed in that sequence, was the best short series of exercises.

- Like their adult counterparts, students are "big arms" conscious but concerned more with overall strength than overall muscular development.

- Weight training on a regular basis has no effect on upward growth.

- Weight training for the shotput and discus has little value unless the athlete works on proper form and explosive quickness.

- Junior high students tend to gain as much as their high school counterparts in strength and muscle size but not as much in bodyweight.

- Most junior high and high school students receive little or no supervised instruction in weight training.

- Most students do not realize what exercise or program of exercises are best for the different parts of the body. The lone exception to this is curls which most students identify as an arm exercise.

- The weakest part in the physique of thirteen- to eighteen-year-old males, including the athletes, is the lower back.

- Students who have weights but no knowledge of weight training tend to do one set of very high repetitions in performing an exercise.

- Many coaches believe that junior high students receive few benefits from weight training, so the activity is not encouraged.

- Many high school coaches know little or nothing about weight training beyond a few basics. They are unable to prescribe specific routines for students.

- All school weight training activities should be supervised by trained personnel.

- Working out every day will not give as good results as working out every other day, especially over a long period.

- Exercises should be done with strict observance of procedure to prevent injuries and insure maximum benefit.

- A wrestling competitor, basketball player, or football player should work out heavily only on weekends during the season. Only light workouts should be attempted during the week.

- In general, sets should be held to three and repetitions to ten on the upper body exercises.

- In general, the heavier the weights the students can handle, the stronger he will become.

- Workouts that last more than an hour and a half are too long for junior high students and may cause them to lose interest in weight training.

- Weight training can go a long way to improve the student's self-image in his most formative years.

Some Weightlifting History

Although there is evidence that people of ancient times lifted objects to get stronger, modern day resistance training began in the late nineteenth century in Western Europe. Early barbells and the shorter handled bars called dumbbells were usually fashioned from a solid piece of iron and, therefore, not adjustable.

The number of exercises used was not as extensive as the variety we do today, but we still use several of the exercises that were developed then. Lifting was not very widespread. Lifting contests were held both in Europe and the United States, but there was no official sanctioning body prior to 1900.

The majority of pre-1900 lifters were heavy-set men, since they believed that the bigger one got, the stronger one got. But some weight-lifters took exception to this "bigger is better" rule. One notable early weightlifting enthusiast was Eugene Sandow, a man who rarely weighed over 180 pounds at a height of 5' 8". Sandow used weights to build a magnificent and strong physique. He was also a reasonably attractive fellow, which helped draw in the ladies when he put on one of his exhibitions. Sandow toured America and Europe putting on displays of his muscularity and strength. He even appeared in the famous Ziegfield Follies. Women were supposed to have fainted when he posed, flexing and swelling the muscles of his well-developed physique. Sandow did much to inspire other men to use weights to become stronger and more muscular and helped dispel the idea that weight men were slow and heavy.

By the end of World War I, adjustable barbell sets had appeared, and various lifting contests were being held throughout Europe and America. The Amateur Athletic Union became the sanctioning organization for weightlifting in 1929. The AAU phased out some of the lifts performed in the meets, leaving only the two hands press, snatch, and clean-and-jerk. These three lifts remained the official standards until 1972, when the press was dropped. The AAU also holds powerlifting meets which consist of the bench press, squat, and deadlift, although all three lifts are not always performed.

In 1940, the AAU sponsored the first official Mr. America contest. Held in Madison Square Garden, it was won by the remarkable John Grimek. Grimek developed one of the most spectacular physiques ever attained; he was also a superb athlete. His ability to pose his physique has never been surpassed. Grimek did much to popularize the Mr. America contest, and he is still very active in promoting interest in bodybuilding and weightlifting activities.

In the 1930s, two venerable bodybuilding publications were also begun: Bob Hoffman's *Strength and Health* and Peary Rader's *Iron Man*. Both men and both publications still exert a strong influence today. Bob Hoffman's York Barbell Club in York, Pennsylvania, did a great deal of touring and promotional work in the 1930s and 1940s to stir enthusiasm for weight training.

Using weights to build strength and muscularity was given a tremendous boost during World War II after military doctors wrote of the excellent results attained with weights in rehabilitating injured soldiers. Soldiers returning home from the war bought or made barbell sets for themselves and their sons.

In the late 1940s, a Canadian named Joseph Weider began to challenge Bob Hoffman for his role as America's best known advocate of weight training. Weider emphasized development of large showy muscles while Hoffman continued to emphasize a more conservative approach to weight training. These two men, their philosophies, and their organizations are strong rivals today.

One cannot conclude this chapter without some comment about America's most famous weightlifter, Paul Anderson. Anderson became an international sensation twenty years ago by lifting weights which no one else could approach. Anderson was the first man to press 400 pounds. He is also credited with a 1,000 pound deadlift and a 1,200 pound squat. Anderson is listed in the *Guinness Book of Records* as the World's Strongest Man, due to his 6,000 pound backlift.

Weight Training and the General Public

Very few knowledgeable people doubt the benefits of weight training. Most people, however, know very little about it, and even less about bodybuilding and weightlifting. Television exposure in the last five years has helped the general public differentiate between bodybuilders and weightlifters, but little is known about the men's lives and their training methods.

Weight training is the use of barbells or machines to increase muscular size, strength, and/or endurance. Weight training is used by secondary schools, colleges, and teams in professional sports to build better athletes.

The word weightlifting is often used in place of weight training, but, technically, it refers to a specific sport. Weightlifting is practiced by perhaps fifty to one hundred people in most American states at any given time. New York, California, and Pennsylvania probably lead the nation in weightlifters. Weightlifting in the United States is carried out in two forms: powerlifting and Olympic lifting. Powerlifting requires relatively little technique and a great deal of strength. Olympic lifting requires a combination of great strength, speed, and coordination. Powerlifters perform the bench press, squat, and dead lift in their contests, while Olympic lifters perform the snatch and the clean-and-jerk. Both types of lifters may have impressive physiques, although powerlifters are generally heavier for their height than Olympic lifters. There are practically the same weight classes in each type of lifting: 114, 123, 132, 148, 165, 181, 198, 242, and superheavyweight. Some powerlift meets also have a 220 pound class.

Bodybuilding is the art of developing muscles to large dimensions while keeping fat at a minimum. This is to insure maximum visible "definition" of the muscle. Many bodybuilders refer to having muscular definition as having "cuts". Some bodybuilders are very strong, others are not, depending on how they train. Most bodybuilders are under six feet tall although some, like Arnold Swarzenegger or Lou Ferrigno, are well over six feet. A few professional bodybuilders are able to make a living with their physiques, but most have a variety of occupations. Although people generally realize that a weightlifter beats another by lifting a greater total amount of weight, they are not sure how one bodybuilder defeats another. Bodybuilding or physique contests are decided on the basis of muscle size, muscle definition, posing ability, and body symmetry. The contestant with the largest muscles rarely wins unless he also has good definition. By the same token, he must have overall development of each muscle group. In other words, each body part—the chest, arms, stomach, legs, shoulders, etc.—must be developed in balanced proportion to one another. This overall balance or symmetry is the mark of all top bodybuilders.

There are at least three organizations which hold physique contests in this country. Since they use the same titles for some of their events, the beginning bodybuilding enthusiast can get confused remembering which "Mr. America" is which. The AAU generally considers bodybuilders who compete outside their organization as professionals, even though they do not always accept money as an award.

The general public usually knows very few of the big "Mr." winners. They just do not have the popularity of sports heroes or entertainers, although they are a combination of both.

John Grimek was reasonably well-known in his heyday. Steve Reeves became internationally known after the release of Joseph E. Levine's "Hercules" and "Hercules Unchained" movies in which Reeves played the title role. Dave Draper, a tall blond physique star, appeared in the movie "Don't Make Waves" as well as in several television shows in the late 1960s. Currently Arnold Swarzenegger, perhaps the world's foremost bodybuilder, has caught the eye of the public with his numerous guest spots on TV talk shows, situation comedies, and specials as well as featured roles in motion pictures.

What does the general public think of the average weightlifter or bodybuilder? What are they really like? Weightlifters have a more favorable public image, since their competitions have a more logical reasoning behind them in the minds of the people. Lifting the most weight seems like a sensible way to compete, like scoring the most touchdowns, goals, or runs. Some people do believe that lifters make poor participants in other sports, which is not true. Some of our nation's strongest men are professional athletes who lift weights to improve their playing ability. These men are capable of very respectable powerlifts and overhead presses.

Bodybuilders are considered by some to be egotistical and very likely homosexual. It is true that some bodybuilders have ego problems, but so do many other athletes and non-athletes. Most are very well-rounded individuals. And the author, in ten years of attending and judging physique contests, has never even heard of a homosexual bodybuilder.

The number of people who train with weights is in the tens of thousands. But, there are only a few thousand competitive lifters and probably less than a thousand competitive bodybuilders in the United States.

What to Expect from Working Out

Many high schools and colleges in the United States have been using barbells or weight machines since the early 1960s or before, yet junior high schools usually do not have weight training facilities. Why? There are several reasons: (1) lack of funds available to buy the equipment; (2) lack of trained personnel to properly supervise weight training; and (3) the belief by the school's coaches or administration that weight training will not benefit most junior high age boys.

In high schools, weight training is usually supervised by the head gym coach who has only a limited knowledge of weight training. It is rare to find a physical educator who is familiar with all phases of weight training. Even so, many students can really benefit from school supervised weight training.

Some of you may have access to a private gym, health club, or health spa for workouts. Some of these clubs have very good instructors while others are staffed by good salesmen and poorly informed instructors. The equipment in a private club is generally better than what a school has to offer. And, properly used, the more equipment available to the student, the better. More equipment allows a greater variety of exercise and increases the chances of your developing the right combination of exercises for maximum benefit.

For those who will be working out at home, there is a special section on home training in the next chapter.

Once a program has begun, one should not expect overnight changes in physique or strength. In fact, much depends upon the age of the trainee as well as other factors as to just how fast results are achieved. The thirteen- to fifteen-year-olds should not expect results as fast as the sixteen- to eighteen-year-olds. All students should notice an increase in strength after the first six to eight workouts. There is usually some increase in muscle size after the first fifteen to twenty workouts.

Please do not try to use the routines of older individuals, or try a routine publicized by some physique star. Chances are his routine is not really like that; and, besides, he has been training for years. Follow the advice of a well-experienced gym instructor or coach. If no one like that is available, the advice in this book or a similar knowledgeable publication should be used as a guide.

If you want great strength or a heavily muscled physique and are willing to work out like a wild man to get it, you may not succeed anyway.

A

B

Squats can be done more safely with a power rack, like Greg Lanter is using here. The metal or wooden support is very popular with professional athletes and competitive power lifters.

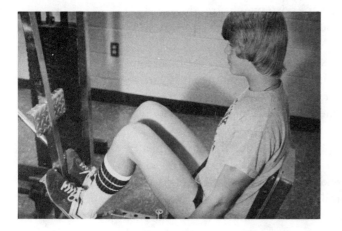
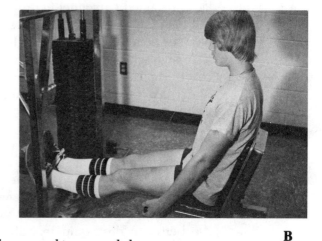

A

B

Jeff Cole demonstrates the leg press with gym machine, a good alternate exercise to the squat.

Unless you are a natural at putting on muscular size and gaining huge amounts of power quickly, building the kind of physique you dream about may take years. After all, how many fifteen-year-olds have seventeen-inch arms? How many seventeen-year-olds can bench press 400 pounds?

Look at the physical size of your father and mother as well as older brothers. Ask your dad and older brother how big they were at your age. This may give you an idea of your potential in getting stronger and heavier. Junior high students may change their appearance drastically before they are eighteen. Students who are juniors or seniors but have slim parents and who are themselves slim may never develop a Herculean physique. However, they still can develop a very pleasing and well-defined build. By the same token a person who is quite heavy with large bones may never develop a highly defined physique.

The question sometimes arises, "Will weight training stunt my

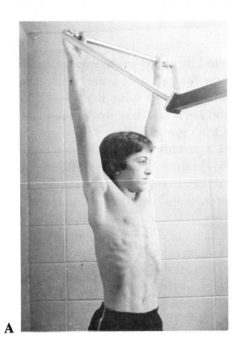

A   B

The chin-up, one of the best free hand arm and shoulder builders, is demonstrated here by Marc Elliott.

In this variation of the bentover row, Pat Smith shows the muscular chest development possible with weights.

growth?" No way, not if you have begun to mature and are experiencing the increased hormone output of most adolescents. The student can tell if he has reached puberty (and most thirteen-year-olds have) by several signs. If the voice has started to change, if sexual maturity has begun, if there is an increase in the amount of body hair, then puberty has begun.

Pre-adolescents, usually under twelve, should be urged *not* to work out because of the stress that weights place on the joints of youngsters.

The author helped several eighth-graders work out some five years ago. These fellows were all athletes then and are now. They worked out for several months at the time. Did it affect their growth? The shortest of the boys then is still the shortest now, but his parents are not tall either. The other boys are all from 5'10" to 6'1" and range in body type from slim-muscular to Herculean in build. Would they have been taller if they had not worked out? Judging by their parents' and brothers' heights, no!

To sum up, *do not* expect miraculous results; but *do* expect results. If there is no increase in strength or size, something is wrong. Perhaps lack of nutrition and rest have affected growth. Perhaps the workout is either too light or too strenuous. Perhaps the exercises are being done incorrectly, or they are the wrong ones. Hopefully, this book can help you avoid some of these mistakes.

Home Workout Needs

If you will be working out exclusively or primarily at home, you will need certain basic pieces of equipment. You should have:

BARBELL

A barbell is usually five or six feet long. All bars of the Olympic Standard type are seven feet long. On your bar you have a sleeve and both inside and outside collars. A sleeve fits around the middle of the bar and revolves. Inside collars separate the weights from the sleeve. Outside collars hold the weights in place.

DUMBBELLS

Two dumbbells are needed. They are usually eighteen inches long. Unless they are of solid one-piece construction, they should have sleeves and collars.

WEIGHTS

Try to have at least ninety pounds of weights. The basic 110 pound set that most stores sell usually has ninety pounds of plates. Plates come in assorted sizes: 2½, 5, 10, and 25 pounds. Some sets have 1½ pound plates while others have 15 pound ones. Olympic Standard barbells come with 2½, 5, 10, 25, 35, and 45 pound weights. Most barbell sets cost from $20.00 to $35.00. Olympic sets cost $150.00 and up, but they are virtually indestructible. Most barbell sets sold today have plastic covered concrete and sand plates. These are cheaper to make and quieter than the all-metal sets. If these plastic covered sets are used heavily, they will last about three years. Additional 25 pound plates should be added to your set as soon as they can be afforded.

BENCH

This item will cost you from $30.00 to $100.00 or more. Why buy a bench? A lifting bench is a padded piece of wood or metal framing about a foot wide and about four or five feet long. It has metal holders attached to it which make it possible to do safer and heavier bench presses. These holders or support racks hold the weights until the lifter is ready to lower the bar to his chest. There is no doubt that a bench will speed up the progress one makes. Bench presses are a must for building muscular size and strength quickly. Several other exercises can also be done with the bench.

SQUAT STANDS

These are metal or wooden posts, weighted at one end with V- or U-shaped holders at the other end. Squat stands make it possible to do deep-knee bends without having two partners put the weight on your back or press the weight behind your head before you can squat with it. Squats or deep-knee bends add tremendous power to the legs and can alter your metabolism so that gaining weight comes easier.

WRENCH

Some type of adjustable wrench should be available for loosening and tightening the collars on your bars.

WRIST ROLLER

This device is in widespread use for developing the grip, wrists, and forearms. To make one, get an eighteen-inch section of a mop or broom handle. Also get five to six feet of rope or heavy twine and a five pound barbell plate. Drill a hole or drive a nail through the center of the stick. Attach one end of the rope securely to the handle. Tie the other end around the five pound plate. Instructions on how to use the device will be given later.

Finding a proper place to work out can be a problem. Do not antagonize your family by working out on the $1,000 living room carpet in the midst of the Early American or Louis XIV antiques. Use your own room, or the family room when no one else is using it. The best place to work out, however, is a garage or basement which is well-ventilated and can be heated in the winter.

It is important to stay properly clothed during the workout. Gym shorts, T-shirt, and tennis shoes will do. Heavier clothing should be worn if the temperature is below 65 degrees. Resist the temptation to work out without a shirt, even on very warm days. Our demonstrators doffed shirts only so you would be able to see the results of proper training.

The Muscles That You Exercise

All living organisms are fascinating; the more complex they are, the more fascinating they become. The human body, because each of us owns one, is particularly interesting. This section takes a brief look at one system of the human body: the muscles.

A detailed analysis of muscle tissue, of the types of muscles, and other such information is not necessary. What is necessary is a close look at why muscles grow, why they respond to exercise, and the identification of muscles.

Just as our body converts food into energy to use as a fuel, the individual muscle cells burn oxygen as a fuel. The better the shape our muscles are in, the more efficiently our muscle cells use oxygen.

When we inhale, oxygen is transmitted from the lungs to the blood system of veins, arteries, and capillaries. These blood vessels carry oxygen to the cells of our muscles. When exercise is performed, the body responds by pumping more blood containing oxygen into the muscles. People who exercise regularly and strenuously develop very efficient cardiovascular systems. That is, their hearts pump more blood with fewer beats to the muscles, thus getting more fresh oxygen to muscle tissue. With more fresh oxygen to convert to energy, the muscle cells and, therefore, the muscles themselves can work longer and more efficiently.

It should be easy to see that the benefits of proper exercise carry over to many daily activities. Having excellent muscle tone and a highly efficient heart (more blood pumped per fewer beats) can make many day-to-day tasks much less tiring.

There are several muscles of the body that are quite visible. Other muscles lie underneath the skin or skeleton or underneath other muscles in such a way that we do not usually notice them. The muscles of men are more noticeable than those of women although both sexes have the same muscular system. Women have a heavier layer of protective fat covering the muscles and do not have the hormone output to produce the same size muscles as men.

The muscles developed in weight training will be discussed in descending order beginning with those of the neck.

NECK

The sternocleidomastoid and other less prominent muscles of the neck respond readily to free-hand exercises and weight-resistance. Wrestling and football coaches work at length to develop strong if not large necks on their athletes to avoid neck and spinal injuries. Neck bridges, pressing the hands against the head for a "10-count," neck harnesses, and towel resistance are popular ways of building these muscles.

BACK

The trapezius is located in a large, trapezoid-shaped area across the top of the back. The trapezius muscle tapers to a point about midway down the spine. Olympic lifters often develop thick, bulging trapezius muscles.

The teres minor and major are two muscles located at the shoulder blades (scapulae) and are developed by shoulder, arm, and back exercises.

The latissimus dorsi is the large back muscle. It extends across the width of the back and gives the male his "V-taper" from shoulders to waist. This muscle, referred to in the plural as the "lats," can be visibly flexed and widened with proper muscle control.

The spinal erectors are muscles which support the spine and help keep it straight. Actually the spinal erectors are only one muscle which divides itself and overlaps. These muscles can be visibly seen to flex in more muscular persons.

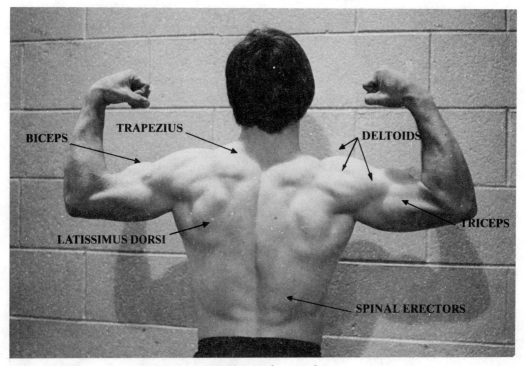

Upper Body—Back.

Notice the heavily-developed muscles along the spine as Carl Betsch performs a handstand.

CHEST

The pectoralis minor and major are two muscles located on each side of the chest which make up the muscular slabs known as the pectorals, attached to the sternum. These muscles, particularly the pectoralis major, can be developed to a thickness of several inches.

The serratus muscles, which are attached to the ribs, are visible at the side of the chest.

SHOULDERS

The deltoids (anterior, posterior and lateral) are the highly visible muscles which "cap" the shoulders. These can be built to enormous size through weight training.

ABDOMEN

The external obliques are muscles running obliquely across the abdomen. They are visible as "side muscles" that seem to frame the rectus abdominis muscles of the front of the abdomen. These are visible in people with small, muscular waists.

The rectus abdominis are muscles appearing in two or three rows

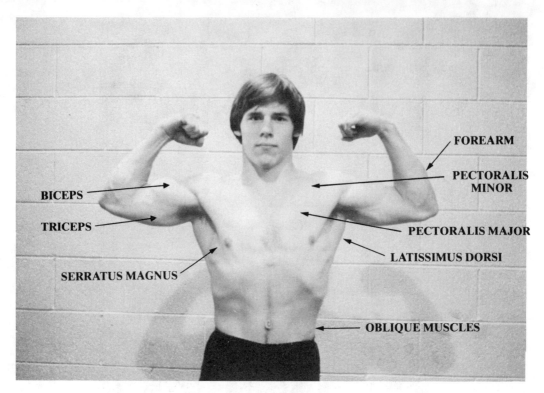

BICEPS

TRICEPS

SERRATUS MAGNUS

FOREARM

PECTORALIS MINOR

PECTORALIS MAJOR

LATISSIMUS DORSI

OBLIQUE MUSCLES

Upper Body—Front.

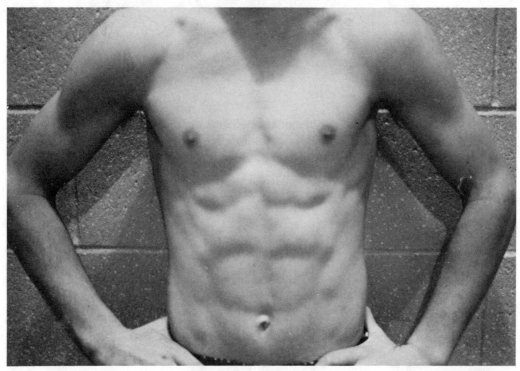

Hixson Junior High wrestler Marc Elliott displays four rows of abdominal muscles.

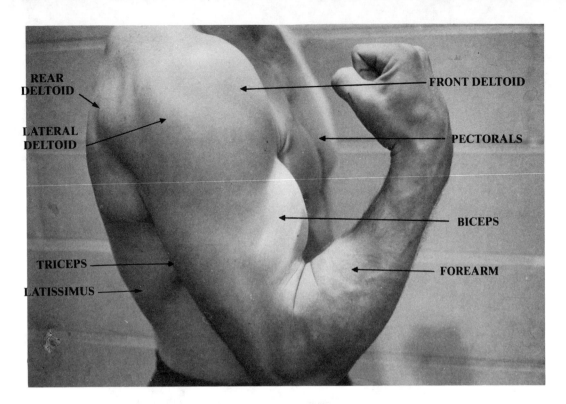

Upper Body—Side.

across the front of the abdomen. Gymnasts, swimmers, and wrestlers as well as bodybuilders have highly defined rectus abdominis muscles. Many junior high and high school athletes have hard, well-defined muscles of this type.

ARMS

The biceps is one of the best known muscles in the body. Most younger teenagers know what to do when someone asks them to "Flex your biceps." The biceps is located in the anterior (front) part of the upper arm and is composed of two heads. When flexed, the biceps may appear long and smooth, it may appear like a chunk of rock beneath the skin, and, more rarely, have a visibly split peak.

The brachialis is a muscle which lies more or less between the biceps and triceps and adds to upper arm bulk.

The triceps is the three-headed muscle located in the posterior of the upper arm. Each of the muscle's three strands originates from a different point and unites to form the main bulk of the upper arm.

The forearms are four major muscles in the anterior of the forearm and six major muscles in the posterior. These muscles act as flexors and extensors for the hand and wrist. The visibility of these muscles under the skin varies greatly.

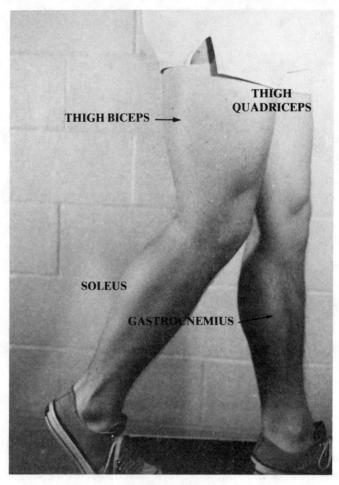

THIGH QUADRICEPS

THIGH BICEPS →

SOLEUS

GASTROCNEMIUS →

Lower Body—Side.

HIPS

The gluteus maximus are the large globe-shaped muscles commonly referred to as the "butt." They are usually covered with a fatty layer. The size of these muscles varies greatly. Slim people sometimes have large, muscular buttocks while large people may have very flattened gluteus maximus muscles. These muscles contribute much to leg power, particularly the kind of driving force useful in football and sprinting. Smaller hip muscles include the gluteus medius and gluteus minimus.

THIGHS

The quadriceps femoris include the rectus femoris, vastus lateralis, vastus medialis, and vastus intermedius. A very large powerful muscle with four sections, it is used for kicking a football and in doing deep-knee bends.

The sartorius is the longest muscle in the body—running from a midpoint along the side of the hip to below the knee.

The adductor longus is on the medial side of the thigh; this muscle is often pulled by sprinters who do not warm up properly.

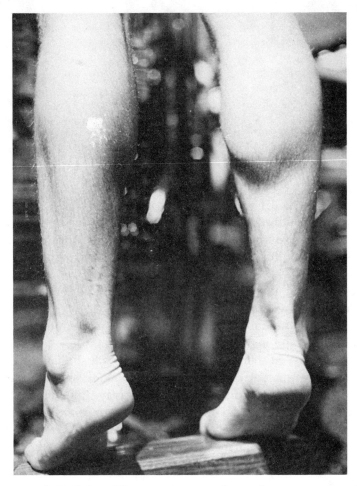

This close-up of Carl Betsch's toe raise reveals good gastrocnemius (inner portion) development of the right calf.

The biceps femoris is a two-strand muscle located in the back of the leg. The biceps femoris along with the semitendinosus and semimembranosus muscles form what are generally called the "hamstrings."

CALVES

The gastrocnemius is the one muscle most visible, and the one which responds best to weight training.

The soleus is the other muscle making up the calf portion of the leg. The soleus can be increased in size through running and specialized weight training.

Sizing Yourself Up

One very good way to check on one's progress in weight training is to take measurements of the muscles. This should be done at the beginning of the weight training program. Later measurements should be taken at intervals of once every twelve to fifteen workouts.

A cloth, vinyl, or steel tape may be used, but be sure it is accurate. A cloth tape may eventually shrink from getting sweaty or from moisture in the air. A steel tape may not follow the curve of the muscle properly. A vinyl sewing tape is probably the best of the three.

Almost every author who has written a book similar to this one has given a different set of instructions on taking measurements. This author's set is no exception and, in fact, may differ more than usual.

First, do not measure yourself. Let a parent or friend do the job to get a more accurate measurement. When measuring ourselves, we all tend to see an extra quarter of an inch where there is none. Strip down to a pair of gym shorts or underclothing and follow this procedure for measuring the muscle groups:

UPPER ARMS

Raise the upper arm until it is at a right angle to your side. Flex your biceps, and triceps too, making sure to bring your clenched fist down toward your shoulder. Pass the tape around the largest circumference of the upper arm. Keep the tape straight. Do not measure diagonally. Measure both upper arms in this manner.

FOREARMS

Turn the palm up with the forearm more or less parallel to the floor and at a right angle to the body. Clench the fist and bend it back toward your elbow. Keep the "belly" or bottom of the forearm facing up. Do not twist the forearm to the side and do not make a "gooseneck" with the forearm. It is too difficult to measure from one time to the next when this is done.

WRISTS

With the palm up, circle the wrist snugly but not tightly with the tape. Be sure that the tape is between the wrist bone and the palm. It should not be on the wrist bone, behind the wrist bone, or on the palm.

CHEST

Bring the arms out to the side and pass the tape around the chest and back about one inch from the top of the armpit. Make sure the tape is straight and snug in the back. Avoid flexing the back's lat muscles or filling the chest with air. Another way of measuring the chest is to measure it across the nipples and below the armpit. Then take the average of the two figures as the chest measurement.

WAIST

Measure the waist by passing the tape across the navel in front and keeping the tape straight along the back and sides.

NECK

Measure the neck in three places and take the average. Measure above, on, and below the "Adam's Apple."

UPPER THIGH

Most books tell you to measure the thigh only below the buttocks. This author prefers both an upper and a mid-thigh measurement. To measure the upper thigh, pass the tape around the thigh below the hip and through the crotch. The leg should be flexed.

MIDDLE THIGH

Measure the length of the thigh from below the buttock to immediately above the knee cap. Take half of that measure and measure the thigh at this mid-point between the hip and knee. The leg should be flexed.

KNEE

Measure across the middle of the knee cap.

CALF

The person having his calves measured should be sitting. He should raise upon one toe while sitting and flex his calf as much as possible. The calf should be measured in several places and the largest measurement recorded.

ANKLE

Measure the ankle directly above the ankle bone.

Remember that measurements are only one guideline to follow in determining your progress. They certainly do not tell the whole story.

Highly defined muscles, well-shaped muscles, and, of course, strong muscles do not figure in a simple measurement of circumference. One should decide from his overall appearance if he is making progress.

Over the years, magazines and books have printed the ideal measurements which a person should have. There are no such things. Due to the length of the bones, the breadth of the shoulders, bone thickness, and other factors, muscles of the same size will not appear the same, even if two people are the same height and weight. A man with seventeen-inch arms who wears a thirty-inch sleeve will generally have more impressive arms than someone of the same size who wears a thirty-four sleeve. The arm will appear thicker and more massive.

Generally, a person whose chest measures seven inches greater than his waist has an athletic build, at least in so far as having a "V-taper." One who has a ten-inch or greater differential between the chest (the larger measurement) and the waist generally has an excellent V-shaped torso and presents quite a manly, if not powerful, appearance. Some bodybuilders have a fifteen-inch or greater differential. The term "V-taper" refers to the rough V-shape of the torso with the shoulders being the top of the V and the waist the closed angle or bottom of the V.

Picking a Suitable Program

Choosing a suitable program seems to be the hardest part of weight training for many young people. Poor or inadequate advice sometimes leads youngsters to use training programs that have little or no benefit.

There are probably as many different successful training programs as there are weightlifters, so it is sometimes hard to say when one routine is better than another. There are several basic rules, however, which will enable almost anyone to set up a successful program, regardless of his physical ability or training objectives.

Select one, but not more than two, exercises for each major muscle group: the chest, back, shoulders, arms, thighs, calves, neck, and stomach. The physiological terms for the muscles are given in another chapter, but these simple terms will do for the present.

Exercise first the muscles which you most want to develop. For example, if a large muscular chest is desired, do bench presses or other chest exercises as the first part of the workout. It will be possible to handle more sets and more weights while still fresh.

You may exercise the muscles in practically any sequence, but one sequence seems to be superior to most others. Try working the chest, then the back, then the shoulders, followed by arm exercises. Leg and stomach work can be done either before or after working those other four areas.

Work out with weights every other day. Leave a day between workouts so that the muscle tissue has time to rebuild. The stress placed on muscles by progressive weight training causes a heavier "break down" of muscle cells than other exercising, and the rebuilding period may take twenty-four hours or longer.

It is especially important for a junior high age student or a slim high school student who is trying to gain weight to rest a day between workouts. In fact, a Monday–Wednesday–Friday training sequence, with a complete layoff on Saturday and Sunday, is advised for those slimmer persons seeking to gain muscular bulk. If you are interested in gaining weight, the worst thing to do is overtrain.

People who have worked out for a year or so and made good progress may want to use a split routine. In order to do more exercising but yet cut down daily workout time, it is possible to work one part of the body one day and another part the next. Exercising the upper body and legs on alternate days is the most popular split routine. Avoid split routines if you are trying to gain a lot of weight. Only quite advanced weight training enthusiasts can usually gain a lot of weight on split routines.

Boys who are exercising to lose weight should work out three days a

A

B

Side twist exercises, either standing up or seated as demonstrated by Mark Moore, firm up and slim down the middle torso. Combined with upper body developing exercises, it will aid in achieving the "V-taper."

week, do calisthenics every day, and diet properly. Running, jogging, and jumping rope will help speed weight loss, but calorie intake control is most important. Following this chest–back–shoulders–arms sequence creates a flow of blood from area to area that seems to promote faster growth. The lifter will also not tire as easily.

Before every workout, whether it is your first or 1,001st, do some stretching exercises before tackling the weights. Toe-touches, shoulder rotations, trunk rotations, and other warm-up calisthenics will help prevent muscle strain and soreness once the work with the weights gets underway.

After choosing the exercises, begin exercising by doing one set of repetitions. A repetition counts as one exercise movement (one curl, one squat, etc.), and a set represents a group of repetitions. Stick to one set for the first three workouts to accustom the muscle to the exercise. After three workouts, try to go to two sets. Stay with two sets for three to six more workouts, then go to three sets. When three sets seem easy, increase the weight being used by ten pounds or more.

Older students who have worked out for several months with good results may do three exercises per muscle group. It is not advisable to add more than this unless one plans to specialize as a bodybuilder or weightlifter.

Along the same line of thought, avoid doing more than three sets unless you've gotten months of hard training under your belt or unless you've been advised to do so by a real expert in the field. Why not start off with three sets instead of one? Some teenagers can—especially with a light training program. However, it is best to condition the muscles gradually. It is not good to subject them to a strenuous routine at the beginning. This increases the likelihood of strain or injury.

Taxing muscles to the limit every workout may cause the person to dread his workouts and give up. Being able to handle the weights from the beginning of the program, without having to fight for each repetition, will put the lifter in a much more positive frame of mind.

Each repetition of each set should be done properly, strictly following the procedure. Avoid cheating on the exercises. Working out fast is fine, but fast in this case means reducing the time of rest not doing each repetition as rapidly as possible.

Rest about one to two minutes between sets and three minutes between exercises.

Avoid exercising the arms first as they may become too tired to allow the remaining exercises to be completed. Save arm work for last.

The amount of weight to use in the training program is determined by how much the beginner can lift without having to strain hard, shake, or cheat to do it. Below is a chart listing the most common exercises and the poundages to start with based on a percentage of your own body weight.

EXERCISE	AGE 13–15	AGE 16–18
	PERCENTAGE OF BODYWEIGHT	PERCENTAGE OF BODYWEIGHT
Bench Press	45	55
Incline Bench Press	30	40
Flying Exercise	10	10
Dumbbell Bench Press	40	50
Behind-the-Neck Press (Seated)	33⅓	40
Behind-the-Neck Press (Standing)	35	40
Military Press	40	50
Bentover Row	25	33⅓
Upright Row	25	25
Deadlift	75	80
Quarter-Squat	100+	100+
Half-Squat	90	90
Full-Squat	65	75
Curl (Barbell)	25	30
Curl (Dumbbell)	20	20
Reverse Curl	20	20
Triceps Extension	20	25
Triceps Extension (lying)	20	25
Bent-Arm Pullover	15	15
Lat Machine Pressdown	20	25
Lat Machine Pulldown	50	50
Leg Extension	10	20
Leg Curl	5	10
Leg Press	75	100
Power Clean	45	60

The following section lists several good general training programs. Other sections of the book have routines to aid in sports, routines for girls, and special programs for bodybuilders and weightlifters.

GENERAL TRAINING PROGRAMS FOR JUNIOR HIGH

Beginning Program   SETS

(1) Bench Presses	3 × 8
(2) Behind-the-Neck Presses	3 × 8
(3) Bentover Rows	3 × 8
(4) Curls	3 × 10
(5) Half-Squats	3 × 12
(6) Toe Raises	3 × 15

Use this program three times per week. Substitute military presses if no bench is available.

Gaining Weight

(1) Bench Presses	3 × 8
(2) Behind-the-Neck Presses	3 × 8
(3) Bentover Rows	3 × 8
(4) Deadlifts	2 × 8
(5) Curls	3 × 10
(6) Half-Squats	3 × 12

Use this program three times per week.

Losing Weight

(1) Military Presses	3 × 10
(2) Behind-the-Neck Presses	3 × 10
(3) Upright Rows	3 × 10
(4) Flying Exercise (Flyes)	3 × 10
(5) Curls	3 × 10
(6) Half-Squats	3 × 15

Work out fast, switching from one exercise to another after one set without rest. Include sit-ups, leg raises, and running every day, if possible.

Advanced

(1) Bench Presses	3 × 8
(2) Flyes	3 × 8
(3) Behind-the-Neck Presses	3 × 8
(4) Bentover Rows	3 × 8
(5) Upright Rows	3 × 8
(6) Curls	3 × 8

	SETS
(7) Triceps Extensions	3 × 8
(8) Half-Squats	3 × 8
(9) Toe Raises	3 × 15

GENERAL TRAINING PROGRAMS for HIGH SCHOOL

Beginning Program

(1) Bench Presses	3 × 10
(2) Behind-the-Neck Presses	3 × 10
(3) Upright Rows	3 × 10
(4) Bentover Rows	3 × 10
(5) Curls	3 × 10
(6) Triceps Extensions Pressdowns	3 × 10
(7) Half-Squats	3 × 12
(8) Toe Raises	3 × 15

Start with one set and work up to three. Do this program three times a week.

Gaining Weight

(1) Bench Presses	3 × 8
(2) Incline Bench Presses	3 × 8
(3) Behind-the-Neck Presses	3 × 8
(4) Bentover Rows	3 × 8
(5) Deadlifts	3 × 8
(6) Curls	3 × 10
(7) Half- or Full-Squats	3 × 12

Work out as heavy as possible. Add triceps extensions after the curls after fifteen workouts.

Losing Weight

(1) Military Presses	3 × 10
(2) Upright Rows	3 × 10
(3) Flyes	3 × 10
(4) Power Cleans	3 × 10
(5) Curls	3 × 10
(6) Half-Squats	3 × 15

Work out fast, switching from one exercise to another after one set without rest. Try running, sit-ups, and leg raises every day. You must also diet.

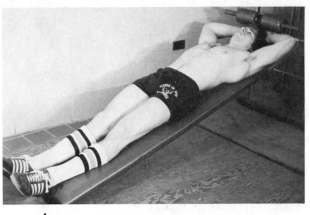

A

B

C

Leg raises may be done lying flat, or on an incline board. Many exercisers consider **B** *as the finish position. Others, like Ronnie Voss, prefer to go higher.*

Advanced	SETS
(1) Bench Presses	3 × 10
(2) Incline Bench Presses	3 × 10
(3) Flyes	3 × 10
(4) Behind-the-Neck Presses	3 × 10
(5) Bentover Rows	3 × 10
(6) Curls	3 × 10
(7) Triceps Extensions	3 × 10
(8) Half-Squats	3 × 12
(9) Toe Raises	3 × 15

Weight Training for Sports

Weight training is widely accepted in athletics as the best way to increase size, strength, and even speed in some sports. This chapter contains numerous weight training programs, some very specific, which should aid the high school and junior high athlete in excelling at his sport or sports.

Most of these are full programs and are meant to be used in off-season. Some athletes may be able to do them on weekends and a few (very few) may be able to work out regularly during the season. Unless otherwise stated, these training programs are meant to be used three days a week, not every day.

Remember, working out with weights and playing a sport at the same time takes excellent conditioning and a high energy level. Both endeavors may suffer if both are pursued.

If the reader fails to find a training program for his particular sport, try using one for a similar sport or devise one from the sound advice in other parts of the book. Girls will find a chapter devoted to them with programs outlined for several sports.

WEIGHT TRAINING FOR SPORTS—JUNIOR HIGH

Football—Lineman

		SETS
(1)	Bench Presses	3 × 10
(2)	Upright Rows	3 × 10
(3)	Bentover Rows	3 × 10
(4)	Behind-the-Neck Presses	3 × 10
(5)	Curls	3 × 10
(6)	Leg Extensions	3 × 12
(7)	Leg Curls	3 × 12
	(Half-squats can be substituted for both the leg extensions and curls).	
(8)	Toe Raises	3 × 15

Optional exercise: Wrist Curls, 3 sets of 5

Football—Running Backs

		SETS
(1)	Bench Presses	3 × 10
(2)	Flyes	3 × 10
(3)	Behind-the-Neck Presses	3 × 8
(4)	Upright Rows	3 × 10
(5)	Curls	3 × 10
(6)	Half-Squats	3 × 12
(7)	Toe Raises	3 × 15

Use this program along with running to get in shape. Run 1–3 miles at least three times per week.

Football—Kicking Specialist

(1)	Bench Presses	3 × 10
(2)	Behind-the-Neck Presses	3 × 8
(3)	Upright Rows	3 × 8
(4)	Curls	3 × 10
(5)	Leg Extensions	2 × 12
(6)	Thigh Curls	2 × 12
(7)	Half-Squats	3 × 12
(8)	Toe Raises	4 × 15

Running up and down steps is highly recommended for alternate days.

Baseball—Pitchers

(1)	Flyes	3 × 10
(2)	Behind-the-Neck Presses	3 × 10
(3)	Upright Rows	3 × 10
(4)	Curls	3 × 10
(5)	Wrist Curls	2 × 10

Baseball—Catchers

(1)	Flyes	3 × 10
(2)	Behind-the-Neck Presses	3 × 10
(3)	Curls	3 × 10
(4)	Wrist Curls	2 × 10
(5)	Thigh Extensions	2 × 12
(6)	Thigh Curls	2 × 12

Upright rows are optional. Half-squats may be substituted for thigh extensions and curls.

Baseball—Fielders

		SETS
(1)	Bench Presses	3 × 10
(2)	Flyes	3 × 8
(3)	Dumbbell Presses	3 × 8
(4)	Upright Rows	3 × 10
(5)	Curls	3 × 10
(6)	Wrist Curls	2 × 10
(7)	Thigh Extensions	2 × 12
(8)	Thigh Curls	2 × 12

Half-squats may take the place of the other two leg exercises.

Basketball

(1)	Bench Presses	3 × 10
(2)	Flyes	3 × 10
(3)	Bentover Rows	3 × 8
(4)	Upright Rows	3 × 8
(5)	Curls	3 × 10
(6)	Half-Squats or Thigh Extensions	3 × 12

Track—Sprinters and Jumpers

(1)	Dumbbell Presses	3 × 10
(2)	Flyes	3 × 10
(3)	Curls	3 × 10
(4)	Thigh Curls	3 × 12
(5)	Thigh Extensions	3 × 12
(6)	Toe Raises	3 × 15

Track—Middle and Long Distance

(1)	Dumbbell Presses	3 × 10
(2)	Flyes	3 × 10
(3)	Curls	3 × 10
(4)	Quarter-Squats	3 × 15
(5)	Thigh Curls	3 × 12

Track—Weight Men

(1)	Bench Presses	3 × 8
(2)	Incline Bench Presses	3 × 8
(3)	Behind-the-Neck Presses	3 × 8
(4)	Upright Rows	3 × 8
(5)	Dumbbell Presses	3 × 8
(6)	Curls	3 × 10
(7)	Triceps Extensions	3 × 10
(8)	Half-Squats	3 × 12

Wrestling   SETS

    (1) Bench Presses   3 × 10
    (2) Incline Bench Presses   3 × 10
    (3) Bentover Rows   3 × 10
    (4) Upright Rows   3 × 8
    (5) Curls   3 × 10
    (6) Triceps Extensions   3 × 8
    (7) Half-Squats   3 × 12
    (8) Toe Raises   3 × 15

Tennis

    (1) Military Presses   3 × 10
    (2) Behind-the-Neck Presses   3 × 8
    (3) Flyes   3 × 10
    (4) Curls   3 × 10
    (5) Thigh Extensions   3 × 12
    (6) Thigh Curls   3 × 12

Swimming

    (1) Bench Presses   2 × 10
    (2) Flyes   2 × 10
    (3) Lateral Raises   2 × 10
    (4) Bentover Rows or Lat
           Pulldowns   2 × 10
    (5) Curls   2 × 10
    (6) Thigh Extensions   3 × 12
    (7) Thigh Curls   3 × 12
    (8) Toe Raises   3 × 15

Water-Skiing

    (1) Bench Presses   3 × 10
    (2) Upright Rows   3 × 10
    (3) Curls   3 × 10
    (4) Wrist Curls   2 × 10
    (5) Half-Squats   3 × 12

Golf

    (1) Bench Press   3 × 10
    (2) Flyes   3 × 10
    (3) Behind-the-Neck Presses   3 × 8
    (4) Curls   3 × 10
    (5) Triceps Extensions   3 × 8
    (6) Half-Squats   3 × 12

Football—Linemen SETS

(1) Bench Presses — 3 × 10
(2) Incline Bench Presses — 3 × 10
(3) Behind-the-Neck Presses — 3 × 10
(4) Power Cleans — 2 × 10
(5) Deadlifts — 2 × 10
(6) Curls — 3 × 10
(7) Triceps Extensions — 3 × 10
(8) Half-Squats — 3 × 12
(9) Leg Curls — 3 × 12
(10) Toe Raises — 3 × 15

Increase weight for each set on the bench press. Start with one set of all exercises and increase to two sets after three workouts. Increase sets to three after nine workouts.

Football—Running Backs

(1) Bench Presses — 3 × 10
(2) Behind-the-Neck Presses — 3 × 10
(3) Upright Rows — 3 × 10
(4) Bentover Rows — 3 × 10
(5) Curls — 3 × 10
(6) Triceps Extensions or Pressdowns — 3 × 10
(7) Thigh Extensions — 3 × 12
(8) Thigh Curls — 3 × 12
(9) Half-Squats — 3 × 12
(10) Toe Raises — 3 × 15

Increase weight on bench press each set. Follow plan of increasing from one set to two after three workouts; then to three sets after nine workouts.

Football—Kicking Specialist

(1) Bench Presses — 3 × 10
(2) Military Presses — 2 × 10
(3) Behind-the-Neck Presses — 2 × 10
(4) Bentover Rows — 3 × 10
(5) Thigh Extensions — 3 × 12
(6) Thigh Curls — 3 × 12
(7) Half-Squats — 3 × 12
(8) Toe Raises — 3 × 15

Baseball—Pitchers

	SETS
(1) Flyes	3 × 10
(2) Behind-the-Neck Presses	3 × 10
(3) Military Presses	2 × 10
(4) Curls	3 × 10
(5) Wrist Curls	2 × 10
(6) Thigh Extensions	3 × 12
(7) Thigh Curls	3 × 12

Baseball—Catchers

(1) Flyes	3 × 10
(2) Military Presses	3 × 10
(3) Behind-the-Neck Presses	2 × 10
(4) Curls	3 × 10
(5) Wrist Curls	2 × 10
(6) Thigh Extensions	3 × 12
(7) Thigh Curls	3 × 12
(8) Half-Squats	3 × 12

Baseball—Fielders

(1) Bench Presses	3 × 10
(2) Flyes	3 × 10
(3) Behind-the-Neck Presses	3 × 10
(4) Upright Rows	3 × 10
(5) Curls	3 × 10
(6) Triceps Extensions	3 × 10
(7) Thigh Extensions	3 × 12
(8) Thigh Curls	3 × 12

Basketball

(1) Bench Presses	3 × 10
(2) Military Presses	2 × 10
(3) Dumbbell Presses	2 × 10
(4) Bentover Rows or Lat Pulldowns	3 × 10
(5) Curls	3 × 10
(6) Thigh Extensions	3 × 12
(7) Thigh Curls	3 × 12
(8) Quarter- or Half-Squats	3 × 12

Wrestling—Quick Program

(1) Bench Presses	3 × 10
(2) Behind-the-Neck Presses	3 × 10
(3) Curls	3 × 10

Wrestling—Endurance   SETS

(1)	Bench Presses	3 × 12
(2)	Incline Bench Presses	3 × 12
(3)	Lat Machine Pulldowns	3 × 12
(4)	Shoulder Presses (Military)	3 × 12
(5)	Upright Rows	3 × 12
(6)	Curls	3 × 12
(7)	Triceps Extensions or Pressdowns	3 × 12
(8)	Leg Presses	3 × 12
(9)	Thigh Extensions	3 × 12
(10)	Thigh Curls	3 × 12

Do one set at a time. Rest no more than fifteen seconds, then go to the next exercise. A good program to follow one month prior to start of the season.

Wrestling—Strength

(1)	Bench Presses	4 × 10
(2)	Incline Bench Presses	3 × 10
(3)	Flyes	3 × 10
(4)	Behind-the-Neck Presses	3 × 8
(5)	Upright Rows or Power Cleans	3 × 8
(6)	Bentover Rows or Lat Machine Pulldowns	3 × 10
(7)	Curls	3 × 10
(8)	Triceps Extensions	3 × 10
(9)	Half-Squats	3 × 12
(10)	Leg Curls	3 × 12

Increase weight each set on the bench presses. Increase weight each set on the behind-the-neck presses. Use as much weight as possible.

Tennis

(1)	Military Presses	3 × 10
(2)	Behind-the-Neck Presses or Dumbbell Presses	2 × 10
(3)	Flyes	3 × 10
(4)	Curls	3 × 10
(5)	Triceps Extensions	3 × 10
(6)	Thigh Extensions	3 × 12
(7)	Thigh Curls	3 × 12
(8)	Toe Raises	3 × 15

Track—Sprinters and Jumpers

	SETS
(1) Dumbbell Presses	3 × 10
(2) Flyes	3 × 10
(3) Curls	3 × 10
(4) Bentover Rows	3 × 10
(5) Thigh Extensions	3 × 12
(6) Thigh Curls	3 × 12
(7) Toe Raises	3 × 12

Track—Middle and Long Distance

(1) Dumbbell Presses	3 × 10
(2) Flyes	3 × 10
(3) Curls	3 × 10
(4) Bentover Rows	3 × 10
(5) Half- or Quarter-Squats	3 × 15
(6) Thigh Curls	3 × 15

Track—Weight Men

(1) Bench Presses	3 × 10
(2) Incline Bench Presses	3 × 8
(3) Dumbbell Presses	3 × 8
(4) Upright Rows	3 × 10
(5) Bentover Rows	3 × 10
(6) Curls	3 × 10
(7) Triceps Extensions	3 × 10
(8) Half-Squats	3 × 12

Swimming

(1) Bench Presses	2 × 10
(2) Flyes	3 × 10
(3) Lateral Raises	3 × 10
(4) Bentover Rows	3 × 10
(5) Upright Rows	2 × 10
(6) Thigh Extensions	3 × 15
(7) Thigh Curls	3 × 15

Gymnastics

(1) Bench Presses	3 × 10
(2) Flyes	3 × 10
(3) Upright Rows	3 × 10
(4) Curls	3 × 10
(5) Half-Squats	3 × 10

Golf

		SETS
(1)	Bench Presses (optional)	3 × 10
(2)	Military Presses	2 × 10
(3)	Behind-the-Neck Presses	2 × 10
(4)	Upright Rows	3 × 10
(5)	Bentover Rows	3 × 10
(6)	Curls	3 × 10

Cross-Country

(1)	Military Presses	2 × 10
(2)	Flyes	3 × 10
(3)	Upright Rows	3 × 10
(4)	Bentover Rows	3 × 10
(5)	Thigh Extensions	3 × 12
(6)	Thigh Curls	3 × 12

Soccer

(1)	Bench Presses	3 × 10
(2)	Behind-the-Neck Presses	3 × 10
(3)	Upright Rows	3 × 10
(4)	Curls	3 × 10
(5)	Half-Squats	3 × 10

You may use the Football—Running Back Program instead.

Canoeing or Rowing

(1)	Dumbbell Presses	3 × 10
(2)	Behind-the-Neck Presses	3 × 10
(3)	Bentover Rows	3 × 10
(4)	Upright Rows	3 × 10
(5)	Curls	3 × 10
(6)	Triceps Extensions	3 × 10

Recommended Exercises

BENCH PRESS
(Pectoral Muscles of Chest)

While lying on the back, take the barbell from the support racks or spotters and lower it to your chest at moderate speed. Let the bar touch your chest, then press it up with considerable force. You will have to decide to what part of your chest to lower the weight. Hold the bar with at least a shoulder-width grip. Many prefer a wider grip. For variation, do bench presses with a collar-to-collar grip or with a close grip, the hands touching each other or almost touching.

A

B

C

Bench Press with Barbell.

A

B

C

Incline Bench Press with Barbell.

INCLINE BENCH PRESS
(Upper Pectoral Muscles, Deltoids of Shoulders)

Incline bench at a 45 degree angle. If the bench has support racks, use those; otherwise, clear the weight to the chest as you sit. Then press overhead. Be careful not to press the weight back over your head, or you may lose control of the weight and drop it behind you. Incline bench presses are easier than standing presses but harder than bench presses.

FLYING EXERCISE
(Pectoral Muscles)

Take two light dumbbells and lie on your back on the bench. Turn the dumbbells so that the palms face each other. Start with your arms straight up overhead with the dumbbells touching. Move the arms, to the sides keeping the elbows just slightly bent to relieve pressure on the joint. Lower the arms until they are parallel to the floor, then raise the arms overhead again. Because this exercise resembles a seal clapping his flippers or a bird flapping its wings, it is nicknamed "flyes."

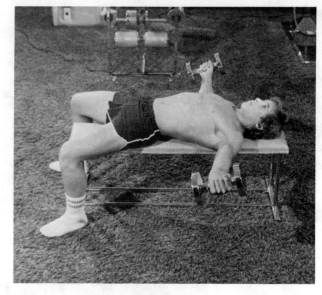

A

Flying Exercise (or Flyes).

B

A

B

Military Press.

A   B

Standing Barbell Press.

The barbell press may also be done seated.

STANDING MILITARY PRESS
(Back, Shoulders, Arms)

Squat down and grasp the bar at shoulder width or slightly wider. Forcibly straighten your legs pulling the weight up from the floor. As it is pulled to chest height, tuck the elbows under the weight and position the weight against the chest. Take a deep breath, and, without bending the knees, push the weight up over the head. The arms should be locked out with the weight overhead. Then, lower the weight to the chest and press it again.

BEHIND-THE-NECK PRESS
(Back, Shoulders, Arms)

Clear the weight to the chest, press over the head, and lower behind the neck. Let this weight rest or touch lightly on the shoulders or back between each repetition. Use shoulder-width grip or wider.

A

B

C

Behind-the-Neck Press.

The behind-the-neck press can also be done in a sitting position, as demonstrated by David Salstrand.

A

B

Power Clean.

POWER CLEAN
(Shoulders and Back)

Squat down and grasp the bar with a shoulder-width grip or wider. Pull strongly using the legs for the initial part of the lift. Pull the weight high on the chest, then tuck the elbows under the bar (a flipping motion), and rest the bar on your chest. Lower the weight to the floor position and repeat.

UPRIGHT ROW
(Shoulders, Back, Chest, Arms)

Grasp the bar with a grip that places the hands six inches or less apart. Stand with the weight hanging at arms' length, then pull the weight up to your chin with the elbows jutting out to either side. Lower the weight to the hanging position; pull up again.

BENTOVER ROW
(Back and Shoulders)

Grasp the bar with grip that is somewhat wider than the shoulders. Stand over the weight with knees straightened and the torso perpendicular to the legs and practically parallel to the floor. Pull the weight to the chest, then lower it to floor. Repeat. This may also be done with a dumbbell.

DUMBBELL PRESS
(Shoulders, Back and Arms)

Load two dumbbells with a moderate amount of weight. Clean the dumbbells to the shoulders. Turn the palms outward so the backs of the hands face you. Press one dumbbell at a time over your head. Alternate for ten repetitions (or reps).

A

B

C

Upright Row.

Bentover Row.

B

Dumbbell Press.

INCLINE DUMBBELL PRESS
(Chest, Shoulders)

Clean the dumbbells to the chest either before or after sitting on the bench. Alternately press them over the head. This exercise should be easier than the standing dumbbell press. For variation, press the dumbbells over the head at the same time.

A

B

Incline Dumbbell Press—Variation.

C

Seated Behind-the-Neck Press.

SEATED BEHIND-THE-NECK PRESS
(Chest, Shoulders, Arms, Back)

Take barbell from racks or clean it to the chest and sit down on bench or chair. Press weight over head, lowering to shoulders each time. Care must be taken not to lose balance while performing this exericse.

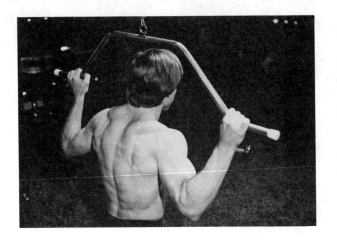

A   B

Pulldown on Lat Machine—Behind the Neck.

PULL DOWN ON LAT MACHINE
(Lats and Shoulders)

A lat machine, sometimes called a dorsi bar, is designed to exercise the latissimus dorsi muscle of the back. These are the "wing" muscles which give athletes the V-taper from shoulders to waist. Grasp the bar as wide as possible. Either kneel or sit, so that, at the top position, the arms are fully extended. Pull the bar behind the head and the back of the neck or shoulders. Let the bar up slowly. Repeat. As a variation, pull the bar to the chest instead of behind the neck.

HIGH PULL
(Upper Back, Shoulders)

This exercise is similar to the Upright Row but the hands' spacing is different. Grasp the bar with a wide grip and stand with it—without cleaning the weight. After standing, pull the weight high on the chest, but do not flip it. Lower the bar to arms' length, but do not place it on the floor. Repeat.

STRAIGHT-ARM PULLOVER
(Ribcage, Chest Muscles, Shoulders)

This exercise can be done on the floor or on a bench. Take a light barbell and place it across the chest. Push weight over head and lower it with the elbows locked and the arms fully straightened behind the head. Pull the bar back over the head with the elbows still locked, and lower the bar to the chest.

A

B

High Pull.

A

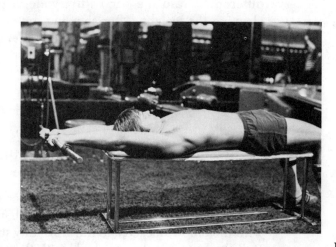
B

Straight-arm Pullover.

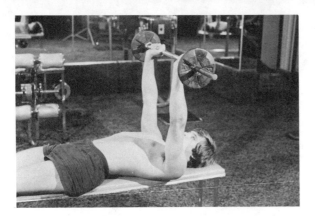
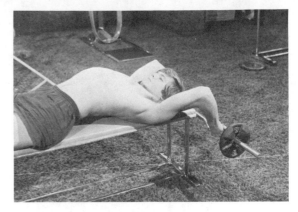

A   B

Bent-arm Pullover.

BENT-ARM PULLOVER
(Chest, Shoulders)

This exercise may be done on the floor or on the bench, but the bench is preferable. A barbell of moderate to heavy weight should be held on the chest with a shoulder-width or narrower grip. Press the weight from the chest like a normal bench press then slowly lower it behind the head. Let the weight touch the floor or come as close as possible, then pull the bar back over the head and lower it down to the chest. That is one repetition. Repeat.

BARBELL CURL
(Biceps, Forearm)

Grasp the barbell at shoulder width with the palms turned face-up. Keeping the elbows into the sides but not touching the sides, curl the weight to the chest. Lower the bar until the arms are hanging relaxed with the bar in hand. Do not keep tensed at this position. Repeat.

A   B   C

Barbell Curl.

Barbell Curl Using Cambered (Bent) Bar.

DUMBBELL CURL
(Biceps)

There are many variations of this biceps exercise. Hold one dumbbell in each hand at your sides. With the palms turned up, curl the weight to the shoulder. You may curl them alternately or at the same time. Curling both dumbbells at the same time is harder.

Dumbbell Curl.

Dumbbell Curl—Alternating.

REVERSE GRIP BARBELL CURL
(Biceps and Forearm)

Grasp barbell with a shoulder-width grip with the palms turned downward. Curl from the waist to the chest. Lower the bar completely unlocking and straightening elbows.

SEATED DUMBBELL CURL
(Biceps, Arms, Shoulders)

This is done while seated in a chair or on a bench. Start with the dumbbells hanging down at arms' length on either side. Curl the weight with palms facing up until dumbbells touch shoulders. Curl both dumbbells at the same time. This requires more effort than Standing Dumbbell Curls.

A

B

Reverse Grip Barbell Curl.

A

B

Seated Dumbbell Curl.

TRICEPS EXTENSION—STANDING
(Triceps)

This exercise works to buildup and enlarge the muscles at the back of the arms. Grasp the barbell with the hands spaced about a foot apart. Clean the weight and press it up over head. Lower the weight behind the head, but keep the elbows close to the head and pointed to the front. Press the weight back over the head using just the triceps. Repeat.

TRICEPS EXTENSION—LYING
(Triceps)

Grasp the bar with the hands about a foot apart. While lying on a bench, press the weight over your head. Lower the bar toward the forehead moving only the forearms. This exercise can be done with either an up or a down palm grip. After lowering the weight to the forehead, press it up, moving just the forearms until the arms are locked out. Repeat.

A

B

Triceps Extension—Standing.

A

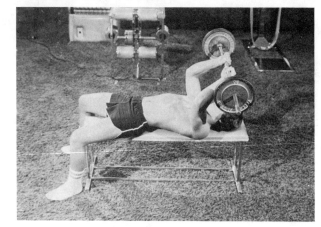

B

C

Triceps Extension—Lying.

TRICEPS PRESSDOWN
(Triceps)

This exercise involves the use of the lat machine. While standing, grasp the lat bar as close to the cable as possible. Press down on the bar with the elbows in close to the sides. Try to keep your upper arms stationary. Press the bar downward until your elbows are locked out straight. Let the bar return to a position where the forearms are parallel to the floor. Repeat. It is important that the lifter not heave his shoulders or otherwise cheat on this lift, in order to handle more weight or reps.

PARALLEL DIP
(Triceps, Chest, Shoulders, Back)

This is a good exercise to finish up a routine but requires special equipment. A pair of parallel bars like those used in gymnastics or a pair especially made for this exercise are necessary. Grasp the parallel bars firmly and push up until the elbows are locked out. Then lower the body as far as possible between the two bars. Again push with the arms and raise the body until the arms are straight. Never let the feet touch the floor. Repeat.

A

Triceps Pressdown with Lat Machine.

B

A

B

C

Parallel Dip.

A   B

Deadlift.

DEADLIFT
(Back, Legs)

This exercise is one of the three power lifts and is also a great strength builder. Squat down, feet apart with a shoulder-width grip or wider. A cross grip may be used where one palm faces up and one faces down. This improves gripping ability. Using the legs and then the back, pull the weight as high off the floor as possible until the back is straight. Throw the shoulders back. Lower the bar to the floor. Repeat.

FULL-SQUAT
(Thighs)

Place the bar across the shoulders. Grip the bar comfortably, but firmly. Squat toward the floor until the midline of the thigh is the

A   B

Full-Squat (Model: Greg Lanter).

A

B

Jeff Cole demonstrates a back-squat, a good exercise to use when squat stands aren't available for regular squats.

prominent depression or furrow running the length of the thigh about halfway between the front and back of the thigh. Do not bounce out of the low position in the squat, but come up at a slow to moderate rate. The full-squat will build the greatest possible power in the thighs and increase their size very rapidly. Full-squats have been criticized for damaging the knees, an unproven accusation. Only those who have very serious knee problems need avoid this exercise. It is important to do this exercise with care, however. Do not bounce out of low position, use too much weight, or twist the knee while performing the lift. Many authorities consider squats the greatest weight-gaining exercise in weight training.

HALF-SQUAT
(Thighs)

Perform this exercise as described for the full-squat, but do not squat below parallel position. This exercise has most of the muscle-building and strength-building benefits of the full-squat but puts less strain on the knees.

QUARTER-SQUAT
(Thighs)

Perform this exercise as described above but squat to a position midway between standing erect and a half-squat. Use more weight for this exercise than for the full- or half-squat. The quarter-squat is a useful muscle builder when combined with other leg exercises. Only by using very heavy weights or by doing very high repetitions is this exercise very beneficial by itself.

A   **B**

Half-Squat.

Quarter-Squat.

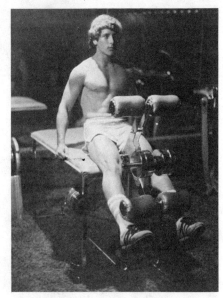

A   B

Thigh Extension.

THIGH EXTENSION
(Quadriceps or Grodricepsor Front Thigh Muscles)

This exercise was first developed for use with iron boots or "health shoes," iron, shoe-like devices strapped to the feet and used by themselves or with added weights. In recent years, machines have been developed which allow safer and more effective use of this exercise. The following description involves the use of such a machine. Sit facing the weight-holding apparatus of the machine. Slip the feet underneath the lower set of pads so that the pressure is on the top of the foot. Lift the leg upward until the knee is locked out straight. Lower the weight slowly, resist the temptation to let the weight apparatus drop.

THIGH CURL
(Thigh Biceps or Back Thigh Muscles)

Lie on the stomach on the thigh extension machine. Slip the feet under the top pads on the machine so the pressure is on the back of the ankle or heel. Pull the weight up and back toward the buttocks. Lower the weight to starting position. Do not jerk the weight upward or let it drop back to the starting position. Development of the thigh biceps greatly aids jumping and running ability. Development of this muscle group gives the thighs a fuller look and makes the buttocks appear smaller. This area of the body is hard to develop through normal exercising or playing sports. Like large calves, thigh biceps seem to be much less common, even among top athletes, than thick chests, large arms, or well-developed front thighs.

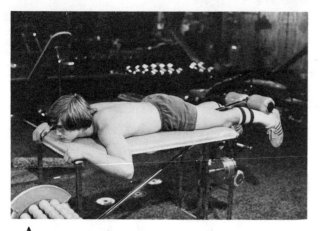
A

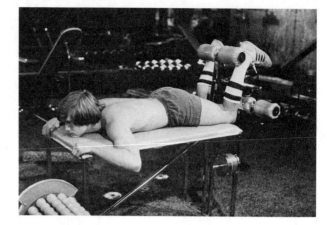
B

Thigh Curl.

A

Jefferson Lift (Model: Jeff Cole).

B

JEFFERSON LIFT
(Thighs)

Here is another thigh exercise also called the straddle lift not requiring squat stands since the bar is lifted from the floor and is not held on the back. Stand straddling the bar with the feet spread fairly wide and the feet more or less perpendicular to each other. Hold the bar at arms' length with the weights touching the floor. This should cause the lifter to be in a half-squat position. Lift the bar using the legs (not the arms) until standing straight. The bar should still be at arms' length. Lower the bar to the floor and repeat the exercise.

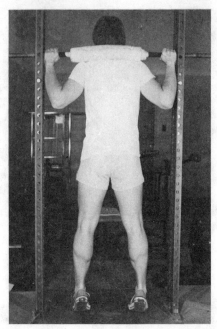

A   B

Toe Raise with Barbell.

TOE RAISE WITH BARBELL
(Soleus and Gastrocnemius Muscles of the Calf)

Place a loaded barbell across the shoulders. Keeping the knees stiff, raise up on the toes. Lower to flatfooted position. For added stretch, stand with the toes on a board with the heels hanging off. Lower the heels until they touch the floor. This exercise should be done in high repetitions to be effective.

DUMBBELL TOE RAISE
(Soleus and Gastrocnemius Muscles of the Calf)

Hold a heavily loaded dumbbell in the right hand at arms' length. Raise up on the toes of the left foot either from the floor or a board. Use the left hand to brace yourself against a wall or door facing. After the left calf tires, place the dumbbell in the left hand and repeat the procedure exercising the right calf.

FREE HAND TOE RAISE
(Soleus and Gastrocnemius Muscles of the Calf)

Brace yourself against a wall or door facing. Using both legs or only one (which is preferable) raise up on the toes from the floor or from a board under the toes. Do high repetitions. No weights are needed.

A **B**

Wrist Curl.

SEATED TOE RAISE
(Soleus and Gastrocnemius Muscles of the Calf)

Sitting on the edge of a chair or bench, place a barbell across the knees. Use a towel or other padding if necessary. Place a board under the toes. Raise up on the toes. Do this exercise slowly and perform high repetitions.

WRIST ROLL
(Wrist and Forearms)

A special apparatus must be made to perform this exercise. Obtain a length of mop or broom handle about a foot and a half long. Drill a hole in the center of the handle. Attach a five or six feet length of rope or string twine through the hole of the handle. Tie a barbell plate to the other end. Hold the handle at arms' length, keeping the elbows straight, and wind the rope until the plate is touching the handle. Unroll the rope. Repeat four times.

WRIST CURL
(Wrists and Forearms)

Sit on the edge of a bench or chair with a barbell placed across the knees. Grasp the barbell, moving the arms under the bar and parallel to the legs. Hold the bar with the wrists and hands turned palms up hanging off in front of the knees. Curl the bar and lower it without raising the arms from the legs. Only the wrist should be used in moving the weight.

LATERAL RAISE
(Deltoids)

Grasp a light dumbbell in each hand. With the elbows slightly bent, raise the dumbbells up from the side and over the head. Let the dumbbells almost, but not quite, touch. Lower to the side. Repeat.

FORWARD RAISE
(Deltoids)

Load two dumbbells with a light to medium amount of weight. With the palms turned down, raise the dumbbells out to the front of the body. Keep the elbows straight or let them bend slightly. Raise the dumbbells to a position over head, then lower to the side. Repeat.

Weight Training for Girls

Although the major weightlifting and bodybuilding magazines have carried articles on weight training for women, most books on weight training ignore the subject. Hopefully, enough topics will be touched on here to enable a young woman, intent on improving herself, to do so with weights.

There are a large number of health clubs and health spas devoted exclusively to women, and most others offer alternate days for ladies' fitness. These clubs generally appeal to those who wish to lose weight, to improve muscle and skin tone, or to build up undersized parts of their anatomy. A young woman athlete who wanted to use weights to improve her agility for a sport would get little help from most health club personnel. The instructors simply wouldn't know how to train for athletics. Their knowledge—and this varies widely—would likely be in the realm of weight loss and control or firming the bust and thighs.

This chapter deals with the traditional reasons women take up weight training and with weight training for athletics.

Many health clubs have a minimum age of sixteen or eighteen at which you may join. Since this book is aimed at the thirteen- to eighteen-year old, some readers may not be eligible to join a health club even if the money to do so is available.

If the reader is of an age to join such a club, the equipment available to her may consist of weights, pulleys, stationary bicycles, belts, rollers, vibrators, etc. Belts, rollers, and vibrators will do very little for muscle tone or weight reduction by themselves. There is no physiological basis for their effectiveness, despite the fact that some very intelligent women will attribute much of their success to them.

Girls who don't wish to or can't join a health club will probably have only two options open to them: work out with weights at home or use facilities available at school or the local community center. Either way, it may be a ticklish situation. At home, it may not be easy to convince male siblings to share their barbells or to talk parents into buying a set for her use. And for many girls, walking into a weight room full of males might be a harrowing experience.

The answer to both situations is—be prepared! Be prepared to state *why* you need the weights. In a gym, you should be able to reel off, to the amazement of any unbelieving males, the exact exercises you plan to do, the number of sets, repetitions, etc. This expertise should throw them off and convince them that you are serious about working out to improve yourself, and they should respond positively. It is advisable, however, to use one or more training partners—for moral support, if nothing else.

Once equipment becomes available, then decide exactly what plan to follow. A good program can be developed from the following exercises and routines.

LOSING WEIGHT AND FIRMING UP

Stomach

Assuming that a good diet is being followed, leg raises, sit-ups, and side twists will help remove stomach flab and firm the midsection. These exercises are done as follows:

SIT-UPS

Lie on the back. Bend the knees to about a 45-degree angle keeping the feet flat on the floor. Place the hands behind the head. Raise the torso from the floor until the elbows can be touched to the knees. Return the torso to the floor and repeat.

LEG RAISES

Lie on the back. Either place the hands behind the head or place the arms on the floor by your sides. Raise both feet, held together and with the legs extended, to a height of about one foot above the floor. Then, spread the legs wide, bring them together, and return the feet slowly to the floor. Repeat.

SIDE TWISTS

Stand erect or sit upright on a stool or bench. Place the hands on the hips. Twist the torso as far as possible to the right and to the left without moving the hips. The exercise can also be done by grasping the ends of an empty bar or a broom handle placed across the shoulders and twisting from side to side returning each time to the forward position.

Do one set of each at first, trying for ten repetitions, eventually increase the sets to three or four and the repetitions to fifteen. A plan may look like this:

	SETS
Sit-ups	3 × 15
Leg Raises	2 × 10
Side Twists	3 × 15

Use a broom handle or an empty barbell across your shoulders to do the twists. Some people find that the twists work better if they sit down while performing each set.

Bust

Many of the same principles in bodybuilding that apply to boys will apply to you. But a girl's build can change dramatically between the ages of thirteen and fourteen. Older girls who have lagged behind may "fill out" in a few short months.

Remember that a girl cannot develop her breasts with weights as they are not muscles but glands. What can be developed are the underlying muscles which tend to give support and lift to the breasts.

The exercises which will give this boost to the bustline are bench presses, flyes, and straight-arm pullovers. If a gym machine is available, the bench presses should be no problem since usually no bar touches across the chest. If a regular barbell must be used, practice lowering the bar to the top of the stomach or just below the neck. See the chapter on exercises for information on flyes and straight-arm pullovers. Start with one set of ten repetitions for each exercise, and add a new set after five workouts. Three sets of ten should be the maximum. Use light weight for fifteen repetitions, if firming without building is desired.

Arms

To firm flabby arms, do curls and triceps extensions or triceps pressdowns with a lat machine. Go for fifteen repetitions and as many as four sets. To build larger arms, use heavier weight and drop the repetitions to eight.

Thighs

If machines are available, by all means do the following exercises to firm and reduce thigh size using light weights.

	SETS
Thigh Extensions	4 × 15
Thigh Curls	3 × 15
Leg Presses	3 × 15

To build larger legs use heavier weight and reduce the repetitions to:

Thigh Extensions	3 × 12
Thigh Curls	3 × 12
Leg Presses	3 × 12

For building or reducing the thighs, ride a bicycle. Cycling is a great way to combine low-cost transportation and life-lengthening, muscle-toning exercise. Running a mile or more at least three times a week will also help firm the thighs.

If only a barbell set is available, round up two spotters and do half-squats. Start with one set of twelve and work up to three sets of twelve. This is for firming or building. To reduce thigh size, start with a light weight for a set of fifteen to twenty repetitions and work up to three sets.

Calves

In order to reduce the size of the calves, run, jog, or ride a bike. In order to build the calves, do the same but include toe raises, either with a machine or with a bar. Refer to the exercise chapter for information on toe raises.

Back

The fatty deposits of the back respond well to dieting and to high repetition lifts that help burn up excess fat and firm the muscles in the back. Try this routine for a slimmer, firmer back.

	SETS
Lat Machine Pulldowns	3 × 15
"Good Morning" Exercise	3 × 20

To do the "Good Morning," place an empty bar on the back and bend forward from the waist as low to the floor as possible. A broom handle will work as well as a bar.

To build a stronger, broader back, try any number of the exercises prescribed in the exercise listings for three sets of eight repetitions. The best bets would be lat machine pulldowns, behind-the-neck presses, or upright rows. Don't do more than two back exercises in the same workout.

WEIGHT TRAINING FOR SPORTS

The exercises recommended to help young men better their athletic performance will work equally well for young women. Listed below are several sports in which girls often participate and some exercises which will strengthen them for those sports. If a more strenuous program is desired, it can be found in the chapter "Weight Training for Sports."

Basketball

	SETS
(1) Bench Presses	3 × 10
(2) Lat Machine Pulldowns or Behind-the-Neck Presses	3 × 10
(3) Curls	3 × 10
(4) Thigh Extensions	3 × 12

Volleyball

(1) Military Presses or Shoulder Presses on Machine	3 × 10
(2) Upright Row	3 × 10
(3) Curls	3 × 10
(4) Thigh Extensions	3 × 12
(5) Thigh Curls	3 × 12

Tennis

(1) Bench Presses	3 × 10
(2) Behind-the-Neck Presses	3 × 10
(3) Curls	3 × 10
(4) Thigh Extensions	3 × 12
(5) Thigh Curls	3 × 12

Shotputting and Discus Throwing SETS

    (1) Bench Presses   3 × 10
    (2) Flyes   3 × 10
    (3) Behind-the-Neck Presses or
              Shoulder Presses   3 × 10
    (4) Curls   3 × 10
    (5) Triceps Pressdowns or
              Triceps Extensions   3 × 10
    (6) Half-Squats   3 × 15

Track

    (1) Flyes   3 × 10
    (2) Curls   3 × 10
    (3) Thigh Extensions   3 × 12
    (4) Thigh Curls   3 × 12

Gymnastics

    (1) Bench Presses   3 × 10
    (2) Flyes   3 × 10
    (3) Curls   3 × 10
    (4) Triceps Pressdowns   3 × 10
    (5) Thigh Extensions   3 × 12
    (6) Thigh Curls   3 × 12

Swimming

    (1) Bench Presses   3 × 10
    (2) Flyes   3 × 10
    (3) Lat Machine Pulldowns   3 × 10
    (4) Thigh Extensions   3 × 12
    (5) Thigh Curls   3 × 12

One good example of how weight training in women's sports is helpful was noted in the 1976 Montreal Olympics. The women's swimming events were dominated by girls from East Germany. Their greater physical strength was evident to those at the Olympic Village and the millions of viewers who watched their gold medal performances on television. The East German women quite readily gave weight training much credit for their speed and endurance. There is little doubt that weight training will play an even greater role in women's sports in future Olympic Games as a result of East German performances.

Group Weight Training

Gym instructors, coaches, and physical education teachers have their own set of problems concerning weight training. The advice and hints in this chapter may be of some help to them as well as students who may be helping their schools organize a class or a course in weight training.

Before the development of the gym machines, which are widely used by schools, training several people at once presented space, equipment, and safety problems. There is no doubt that students benefit as much or more from using barbells rather than machines, but the problems still prevented many schools from setting up group training. Finding space to train as few as ten people has been difficult for some coaches. Providing the bars, plates, wrenches, collars, and wooden platforms or mats to lift on for ten people can also tax the gym department budget. Finally, being able to supervise ten people at once and prevent horseplay, weights from working loose, and to see that exercises are done properly is difficult. Of course, these problems double and triple if twenty or thirty people try to work out!

Here are some tips on training groups with conventional weights:

- Platforms are a must since sooner or later weights will be dropped hard on the floor. Unless the school administration doesn't mind nicks in the concrete or the tile, build some wooden platforms to lift on. Four-by-eights should be strong enough to withstand years of use. Cover the entire weight room floor if possible. Nail or bolt the boards together at 90 degree angles to another board at the top and bottom of the platform.

- Buy cast iron or steel plates and solid metal bars. The sandfilled or concrete-form plastic covered weights are fine for home use but tend to crack or split with hard, constant use.

- Get the school's shop department to make as many benches and squat stands as possible. These can be made from wood or metal.

- Set up stations for everyone to use. Have one station for curls, one for bench presses, one for squats, and so on. Have each student do one set and then change to another station and exercise.

- Unless there is plenty of time and not many people, have a fixed amount of weight on each bar for each student to use.

- If space and equipment are available, have a light and a heavy bench press, military press, or squat station. This will enable the stronger boys to get a good workout without having to change the weights each time.

- Allow no rest time between sets or no more than thirty seconds.

- Always use collars on the ends of the bars. Having weights slide off an unbalanced bar is dangerous.

- Try to have at least five exercises and no more than ten for the students to do. Plan at least one exercise each for the chest, back, shoulders, arms, and legs. Stomach exercises will likely be done without weights.

- After the entire class has finished the circuit from station to station (hence the name "circuit-training" for this type of exercising) more advanced students should be allowed to train on their own.

Training with a gym machine eliminates some of the problems in group weight training. The machines will train six, eight, ten, or more people in a small amount of space. The weights are attached to pulleys and levers and aren't free to drop on heads, backs, chests, and toes like conventional weights. However, careless or thoughtless students can still injure themselves or others through improper use of the machine, so training should be well supervised.

The weight load for any station of a machine can be changed quickly by changing a pin in the stack of weights to another position.

A ten-station machine, including the cost of freight and of setting it up, will exceed two thousand dollars—a healthy investment for any high school athletic fund. The price of setting up a ten-station weight room, including benches, squat stands, wooden platforms, bars, and plates, would cut that cost in half.

Use the same programs listed in other parts of the book for individuals. The only difference will be the order in which each exercise is performed and that the exercises will be done only one set at a time.

Competitive Weightlifting

Only those who are at least sixteen and have no less than six consecutive months of weight training should attempt the programs in this chapter. Setting the stage for branching from weight training to physical fitness or athletics, here are suggestions on how to train with weights when thinking seriously of competitive weightlifting and body-building.

It has been stated previously that despite years of research and experiments, weight training has yet to become a "science." There are too many variables. There are too many different programs that work well. This is just as true in the advanced stages of weight training as it is in the earlier and more general phases of the activity. The training programs that are about to be outlined are based on combinations of exercises that generally work very well. However, one may run across other programs which work just as well.

OLYMPIC WEIGHTLIFTING

Only two of the three original Olympic lifts are now practiced: the clean-and-jerk and the snatch. To be an excellent Olympic lifter requires coordination and flexibility as well as strength. A good coach is almost a necessity in order to become a nationally prominent Olympic lifter. This is not true of powerlifting or bodybuilding.

The Olympic-style lifter should practice the two lifts, the phases of the two lifts, and exercises which correspond closely to the two lifts. He should also work on improving his timing and building his strength.

TWO-HANDS SNATCH

The two-hands snatch is performed by lifting the bar up and over the head in one motion. When the lift is completed, the lifter should have the weight over his head with his arms locked, feet in line, and body motionless. There are two styles in this lift: the squat and the split. In the squat style, the lifter pulls the bar high on his chest then drops into a squat position while driving the bar out to arms' length over his head. The split snatch is accomplished by the lifter's throwing one leg to the front and one to the rear thus lowering his body while forcing the bar upward with the power of his upper body.

76

CLEAN-AND-JERK

The clean-and-jerk is performed by pulling the bar high on the chest. Then, as the bar is flipped or cleaned and the elbows are tucked in, the lifter will drop into a squat or split position. Most lifters do a squat clean in preparation for the jerk. With the bar positioned high on the chest and the body erect, the lifter then does the second part of this lift—the jerk. He thrusts one leg to the front and one leg to the rear, lowering his body while shoving the bar upward without stopping until his feet, in line, steady his body and await the judge's signal to lower the bar.

Here are some of the more common exercises done by Olympic lifters. Exercises not previously defined will be described.

CLEAN-AND-JERK

SNATCH

REPETITION CLEAN
(Bring the weight just to the chest.)

SQUAT CLEAN
(Pull the weight to the chest by squatting under it.)

POWER CLEAN
(Bring the bar to the chest without going into a squat or split position.)

DEAD HANG CLEAN
(Bring the bar to the chest without placing it on the floor or rack each time.)

HIGH PULL
(Pull the bar high on the chest without dipping under it.)

JERK FROM THE RACK
(Do not clean the weight but remove it from the support stands and then jerk it.)

MILITARY PRESS
(Press the bar overhead without using any backbend, shoulder heave, or knee kick.)

SQUAT
(Do half- or full-squats with heavy weight for several sets.)

POWERLIFTING

Powerlifting consists of three lifts: the bench press, squat (deep-knee bend), and deadlift. Powerlifting is most popular in the United States with the number of powerlift meets equalling or exceeding the number of Olympic meets.

Powerlifters train to become as strong as possible since their three lifts require mostly great strength. Powerlifters are usually more massive than either Olympic weightlifters or bodybuilders. They also tend to be somewhat shorter individuals. Some lifters successfully combine body-building and powerlifting training and compete in both types of events.

Many athletes who want to develop the maximum amount of strength possible through weight training use powerlifting routines. A typical powerlifter's program involves lots of sets, with low reps and heavy weights.

Some of the more common and result-producing exercises for power-lifting are listed below.

Bench Press

These are often done in sets of six or less repetitions. Many routines involve a decrease of one to two repetitions as the weight is increased. Example: 1×10 with 135 pounds; 1×8 with 185 pounds; 1×6 with 225 pounds; 1×3 with 250 pounds; and so on.

Incline Bench Press

This exercise helps add to the basic strength of the shoulders, upper back, and chest. It also improves the lifter's bench pressing ability.

Behind-the-Neck Press

This is a favorite exercise of football players and wrestlers for increased shoulder strength. Again, powerlifters do them to help their bench press.

Upright Row

Another favorite of athletes needing great shoulder and trapezius strength is the upright row. This helps powerlifters with the bench press and deadlift.

Full-Squat

This exercise is the only way to develop outstanding leg strength. The full-squat is a must for powerlifters since they must perform it in competition.

Quarter-Squat

Some lifters barely bend their knees and call it a quarter-squat; others may do almost a half-squat and say it is a quarter. Doing quarter-squats with spotters or with power racks enables the lifter to support and lift several hundred pounds more than he can when doing a full squat.

Deadlift

This exercise builds up the entire body. The muscles in the arms, chest, back, stomach, legs, shoulders, and neck will all benefit from this exercise.

Stiff-legged Deadlift

This is a variation of the standard deadlift and differs only in that the knees are not bent, but kept straight to allow the upper body to do all the work.

Triceps Exercise

Many powerlifters like to do these exercises as well as pressdowns, French curls, dips, etc. These triceps specialization exercises build strong triceps, a valuable aid in getting a respectable bench press.

Shoulder Shrug

This exercise is a back and neck builder and aids in creating a strong final pull in the deadlift.

Powerlifting is more popular in the United States than anywhere else in the world. Powerlifting has many more participants in the United States than Olympic lifting even though it is a much newer sport. This is true because powerlifting competition is easier to train for, and powerlifting exercises also benefit the bodybuilder and the athlete who is building size and strength.

Because of the great stress that the heavy weights used in powerlifting place on the muscles and joints, participants must be at least sixteen years old. Younger lifters might run the risk of injury to their immature skeletal structure.

Current top super-heavyweight powerlifters can bench press over 600 pounds and squat and deadlift over 900 pounds.

Bodybuilding

Developing strength, endurance, and a good physique are possible for almost all students who use weights. Developing large, impressive muscles is a much harder endeavor and calls for even more dedication and self-discipline. Diet and rest as well as the choice of exercises assume even greater importance. Despite the claims of some bodybuilding publications, not everyone can develop large, highly defined muscles. They may develop a large smooth looking physique or a slim, highly defined one but never seem to be able to combine the two features.

How does an advanced bodybuilder train? In many ways. One Mr. America contender may use several different but effective programs to reach the top. One program may help him reach a certain stage of development and then lose its result-producing effect. Just as a student may reach a sticking point or plateau in growth or strength, so may an advanced bodybuilder.

Many bodybuilders eventually find the right combination of exercises, those that always give them excellent results. It may be necessary for them to just alter the sets and repetition and weight they use. Other exercises will have been eliminated from the program because they do not give fast or noticeable results.

Advanced bodybuilders use more specialization. They do more exercises that work specific muscles in specific ways. After building a physique which may look great to the general public, these fellows will work to strengthen any weak points that might hurt them in a physique contest.

While competitive bodybuilders tend to use higher repetitions than competitive lifters, that is not always true. Weights used are also variable. Some men can build astounding muscle size with rather light weights and, therefore, are not very strong. Others use very heavy weights and can perform impressive feats of strength. Most "authorities" generally agree that building muscle tissue with moderate to heavy weights without excessive high repetition "pumping" creates a longer lasting physique. Then again, many bodybuilders may use relatively heavy weights with some exercises such as bench presses and squats and rather light weights for curls or triceps extensions.

The following exercises are some of those commonly done by the competitive bodybuilder:

BENCH PRESS
Usually done in many sets and often with a regular, close, and wide grip.

80

INCLINE BENCH PRESS
Used to develop the upper chest and the shoulders.

DECLINE BENCH PRESS
The head is placed lower than the feet. The exercise shapes and develops the lower pectorals.

FLYES
Performed in several sets to develop striations (lines) in the muscle and to chisel out the muscle shape. Flyes may also be done in incline and decline versions. Some advanced bodybuilders do not use the full range of movement in the exercise in an attempt to keep constant stress on the pectoral muscle.

BEHIND-THE-NECK PRESS
This exercise may be done standing or sitting.

Ronny Voss' shoulder muscles are defined through the tension of a seated half-press.

The concentration curl is done slowly and with full attention to the muscle movements.

DUMBBELL PRESS
Done either sitting down or standing up, many bodybuilders do a half-press to keep constant tension on the shoulders.

LAT PULLDOWN WITH LAT MACHINE
For a wide thick back.

CURLS
There are many variations to this exercise. The "preacher bench" curl and the concentration curl are two popular ones. Curls with special bars are also popular. These exercises are designed to work the biceps from different angles and positions for maximum growth. Advanced bodybuilders give as much or more emphasis to the triceps as the biceps. Most students who use weights do not.

TRICEPS EXERCISES

Competitive bodybuilders are always anxious to build the arms as large as possible. Without weight training, the triceps or "back" part (from a hanging position) of the arm composes two-thirds to three-fourths of the arm's mass. It is logical, then, for a knowledgeable bodybuilder to emphasize triceps exercise since this muscle has the greater potential for size. The most common arm exercise, curls, activates the triceps to some extent, so that those who do only curls also work the triceps. However, specific triceps exercises have been developed over the years which activate the muscle fiber much better. Most of these exercises isolate the triceps; that is, they put most of the work of the exercise on the triceps. Standing, lying, or sitting triceps extensions (French curls) are good examples. With cable machines, one may perform triceps pressdowns, close-grip bench presses, hands together push-ups, and parallel dips. These are also beneficial triceps exercises.

FOREARM EXERCISES

Some bodybuilders do none, believing that other arm exercises will also build forearms. Other bodybuilders use wrist curls and the wrist roller, hand grippers and other spring devices to build the forearms.

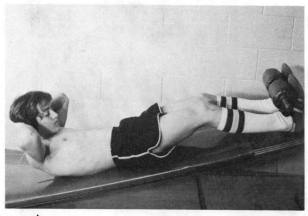 

A   **B**

Marc Elliott performs a sit-up on the incline board. Notice that his knees are bent at the low position.

STOMACH EXERCISES

Proper diet has as much to do with the small waist of a bodybuilder as exercise, but the development of the abdominal muscles comes from hard exercising. Most students who read this book may not need as much stomach work as a bodybuilder in his twenties or thirties. It is much more difficult for an adult to maintain an extremely muscular mid-section because fat collects in that region more easily at a later age. Leg raises and sit-ups are the two basic stomach exercises. Bodybuilders do exercises which are variations of these. Roman chair sit-ups, for example, are done by hooking the feet under a support and leaning back from a sitting position on a pad or seat so that the torso drops below parallel to the legs.

Incline sit-ups are done by lying on a board inclined so that the feet are higher than the head. Another popular form of sit-up calls for the knees to be bent so the thigh and calf almost touch. The torso is brought in contact with the thigh on each repetition but never touches the floor until the last repetition.

LEG EXERCISES

The most advanced bodybuilders follow a program of squats, thigh extensions, thigh curls, and toe raises for all-round leg development. The squats are usually quarter- or half-squats because there is a common belief that full squats cause the buttocks to grow larger.

Many bodybuilders never bring their thigh and calf development up to par with that of their upper body. Nationally prominent bodybuilders, however, have large, well-shaped and proportioned thighs and calves that are amazingly muscular.

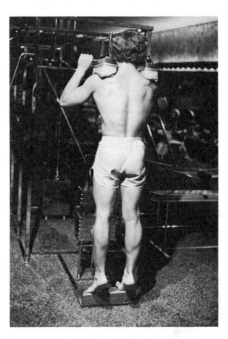

Sixteen-year-old David Salstrand's extremely wide back is evident here as he performs toe raises with a machine instead of a barbell.

Bodybuilders watch their diets more closely than probably anyone— even wrestlers. Bodybuilders often attempt to get 250 to 300 grams of protein per day but there is some doubt as to whether the body actually can utilize that much protein. These advanced weight men do become experts in weight control, and many have the ability to build muscular size while reducing the waist size.

There is no doubt that for many years bodybuilders have had a less-than-satisfactory image. Part of this poor image is due to the public's misconception about the bodybuilder. Many people still have the impression that bodybuilders have little time for anything but training, and that their lives revolve completely around developing more muscle.

This is probably true of some, but many "muscle men" hold down responsible jobs and maintain a well-balanced life which includes family and friends as well as bodybuilding.

The other contributing factor has been the bodybuilders themselves. Strutting along a beach half-flexed or wearing tight T-shirts in the wintertime, they are not likely to make a positive impression on the general public.

Some bodybuilders have helped give advanced muscle building a better reputation. John Grimek, the 1940 and 1941 Mr. America, was an outstanding combination of spectacular muscle, excellent athletic ability, and engaging personality. Many who met him formed a very positive impression of bodybuilders. At one time Grimek virtually stood alone as the nation's outstanding physique star. Crowds would gather just to gaze at him when he went to the beach.

Steve Reeves, Mr. America of 1947 was one of the handsomest title winners. His good looks and superbly proportioned build eventually led to the starring roles in several Italian "muscle" movies. These involved Reeves as a figure of mythology, usually Hercules, who would perform feats of great strength in conquering the villains.

Arnold Swarzenegger has been the leading bodybuilder of the 1970s. He has boosted the image of bodybuilders. Arnold has displayed intelligence, tact, and dignity in numerous interviews in the national media. His portrayal of a Mr. Universe contestant in a film called "Stay Hungry" was well received by critics. Swarzenegger's most recent film to date is "Pumping Iron" a movie adaptation of the highly successful book of the same title.

Bodybuilders who compete in physique contests represent only a small number of the people who could be classified as advanced bodybuilders. Some don't care to pose in front of crowds. Some lack the symmetry needed to win contests. And others don't wish to remove chest, leg, and surface arm hair in preparation for a physique contest.

This author recommends that readers attend at least one physique contest, preferably at the state level or above. When a contestant steps under the posing lights and goes through a minute or so of skillful exhibition of massive muscularity, it can be very impressive.

Athletic Injuries and Therapy

WEIGHT TRAINING INJURIES

The most common injuries that occur in weight training are shoulder and back injuries. These injuries usually occur for two reasons: too much weight is attempted in a lift or the lift is performed improperly. Other injuries that sometimes occur are knee injuries, facial injuries, and chest injuries. No muscle area which may be used in weight training is completely free from possible injury, although injuries of any type are rare. Competitive lifters probably have a higher injury rate than other participants in weight training because they must move large amounts of weight with great speed.

Shoulder injuries may occur from attempting bench presses, military presses, behind-the-neck presses, or any other lift calling for a large amount of shoulder involvement. Shoulder injuries in weight training are generally limited to the deltoid muscles. They should be treated for the first two days or longer with *cold* ice packs, ice wrapped in a towel, etc. The injured area should be rested from three days to a week or longer. If the deltoid area swells or gets extremely tender to touch, a physician should be consulted, particularly if much pain is present.

Back injuries generally result from overhead lifts and most of the injuries are to the lower back. Doing the military press, behind-the-neck press, upright row, high pull, deadlift, clean-and-jerk, snatch, or squat may lead to back pain. Remember that a normal, hard workout may leave the back sore; but if the soreness extends past a day or two, some injury might have occurred. Remember too that if the poundage is right and the form is right, you're home safe; the workout will be injury free. Painful back injury, especially if swelling is evident, should be treated by a physician. Minor back pain can be treated with ice for at least forty-eight hours and then heat in the form of a whirlpool, heat pad, or hot bath.

At one time most muscle strains were treated by heat application. Physiological research in recent years has led athletic trainers and physicians to advocate the use of cold treatment over heat in many cases. Ice treatment has the effect of numbing pain and slowing down any bleeding of the muscle (hemorrhaging) that might take place. When the cold is removed, the body quickly seeks to warm the area and produces a natural heating effect that approaches the healing value of external heat application.

One of the most controversial lifts in weight training is the full-squat. Many coaches believe that full-squats stretch ligaments around the knee and otherwise bring about knee problems. Any dedicated lifter will say that squats are perfectly safe if they are done properly. If full-squats are done fairly slowly, with no bouncing out of the low position and without excessive strain, they should never cause any problems. Half-squats or quarter-squats represent even less risk. A knee injured in weight training should be checked by a physician if there is evidence of swelling or if pain is rather intense. If only some slight pain occurs but persists, the lifter might try wrapping the knee with an elastic bandage before lifting again. Apply ice to the knee for twenty minutes at a time up to three times a day.

Facial injuries are most common in overhead lifts and bench presses. They usually occur when the weight training enthusiast cannot control the bar; the weight is too heavy, the grip is lost, or a blackout occurs. Blackouts due to lack of oxygen are a phenomenon that happens more in Olympic lifting than in other lifting activities. Olympic lifters have dropped bars on their head, back, or chest as they blacked out. Such blackouts are very rare, however. A more common injury is caused by the lifter dropping a bar on his face while bench pressing. Using some common sense in picking the proper weight, using magnesium chalk to insure a good grip, and breathing properly should prevent facial injuries in weight training.

Chest injuries may occur from dropping a weight on the chest or from tearing one of the pectoral muscles. Even a small tear of the pectoralis major or minor from the sternum or shoulder can cause a great deal of discomfort and pain. Such a muscle strain often heals slowly, and impatient lifters often reinjure the muscle by resuming training too quickly. Treatment consists of resting the muscle as much as possible and applying ice for forty-eight hours or longer. After that, heat, preferably wet heat, can be applied if desired. Severe pain and swelling could be evidence of a bad strain, and a doctor should be consulted.

WEIGHT TRAINING FOR REHABILITATION

Physicians often recommend the use of weights to rebuild injured knees, thighs, arms and wrists. The therapy programs outlined below should be of great benefit in rehabilitating areas that have been weakened by injury and lack of use after surgery.

Knee

Use your physician's recommendation about when to begin weight training. For the first week, work out every day without weights on a thigh extension–curl machine. Do three sets of fifteen or twenty repetitions. For the second week, use 2½ or 5 pounds of weights. Work out once a day for three sets of fifteen repetitions. Continue to add five or ten pounds every five workouts after the second week until full recovery occurs. Be sure to do both thigh extensions and thigh curls. Less weight may be needed for the thigh curls.

Thigh

(Quadriceps or Biceps Femoris)

PROGRAM	EXERCISE	SETS	WEIGHT
First Week	Thigh Extensions	3 × 20	no weight
	Thigh Curls	3 × 20	no weight
Do this first week program every day or even twice a day.			
Second Week	Thigh Extensions	3 × 15	2.5 to 5 lbs.
	Thigh Curls	3 × 15	no weight
Third Week	Thigh Extensions	3 × 15	5 to 7.5 lbs.
	Thigh Curls	3 × 15	2.5 to 5 lbs.
Fourth Week	Thigh Extensions	3 × 15	10 to 20 lbs.
	Thigh Curls	3 × 15	5 to 15 lbs.
Fifth Week	Thigh Extensions	3 × 15	20 to 40 lbs.
	Thigh Curls	3 × 15	15 to 30 lbs.
Sixth Week	Thigh Extensions	3 × 15	40 + lbs.
	Thigh Curls	3 × 15	20 + lbs.

Full recovery will have occurred in most cases by the sixth week of rehabilitation and even sooner in some cases.

Arms

Most upper arm injuries respond well to curls, especially broken arms that have shrunk while healing. Triceps pressdowns using a lat machine or triceps extensions using a bar can be very helpful. Once the physician has given his approval, try the following program.

WORKOUT NUMBER	EXERCISE	SETS	WEIGHT
1 to 3	Curls	1 × 15	bar only
4 to 6	Curls	2 × 15	5 to 10 lbs.
7 to 9	Curls	3 × 12	10 to 15 lbs.
10 to 12	Curls	3 × 12	15 to 25 lbs.
13 to 15	Curls	3 × 10	20 to 30 lbs.

Do the program, as outlined above, three times a week. You may work out twice a day for the first nine workouts, thereafter no more than one session a day. After the sixth workout, you may add some triceps pressdowns or extensions to the program. Proceed at a reasonable pace, after the fifteenth workout, until your arm has regained its full strength.

Forearms and Wrists

To rebuild a broken or sprained wrist and an injured forearm requires quite similar programs. There is not much muscle in the wrist but the muscle that is there and the muscle in the hand can be rebuilt through wrist curls or wrist rolls. Start by using just a bar for wrist curls. Add about five pounds every three workouts until full strength has been developed. If a wrist roller is available, start with 2½ pounds on the rope and work up to ten repetitions. Do this exercise every day.

To rebuild the forearm, the program cited above for the upper arm will be quite beneficial. Wrist curls or the wrist roller should also be used. Try this program for forearm rehabilitation:

WORKOUT NUMBER	EXERCISE	SETS	WEIGHT
1 to 3	Wrist Curls	3 × 15	none
4 to 6	Wrist Curls	3 × 12	5 to 10 lbs.
7 to 12	Wrist Curls	3 × 10	15 to 20 lbs.
4 to 12	Wrist Rolls	1 × 8	2½ to 5 lbs.

Questions and Answers

Additional important information is given here in question and answer form. These items include those questions most frequently asked by potential weight training students, advanced weightlifters, and others.

How old should I be before I start weightlifting?

Actually, boys of practically any age can use barbells if the weights are light and present no undue strain on the joints. Generally, for early maturers, twelve is a good age to start, although thirteen to fourteen is soon enough for most.

Is there a limit to how much muscle I can put on?

Yes, there is. How muscular you can become depends upon: age, bone structure, metabolism, and proper program. It is easier to gain strength and muscular size if you: (1) are over fifteen; (2) have a medium to heavy bone structure; (3) gain weight easily; and (4) pick a program which strikes the proper balance between achieving muscular size, strength, and endurance. You may get some idea of your growth potential by looking at your father or at pictures of him when he was in his twenties. Older brothers may give some indication to your size potential.

Should I take protein supplements?

Yes. The average adult is supposed to need sixty grams of protein a day. As a vigorous, active, growing young person, you should aim for 100 grams a day. As stated elsewhere, protein is the basic element necessary to build muscle. However, the body will simply pass through any excess protein it cannot use. Do not waste food and money by taking 300 to 400 grams a day. One hundred to 150 grams per day should be plenty for most teenagers on a vigorous weight training program. Protein powder is cheaper to use than tablets and has a higher protein content per unit of weight.

Should I take anabolic steroid drugs?

No. No teenaged weight trainee or weightlifter should use anabolic steroids. These are drugs which supposedly cause protein to be better assimilated into the body's system. They cause the body to retain more nitrogen and more water in the tissues. A person who takes the drugs on a regular basis will supposedly gain muscular size and muscular strength faster than someone who does not take the drugs. Anabolic steroids are taken by many athletes who want to gain weight faster. Some spectacular results have been claimed for these drugs while some people who have used them have said they have no affect.

Scientific research has shown that this type of drug used by students not completely grown may cause premature hardening of the bone endings. Any person who is still growing might find that growing stopped from the use of these drugs. This is to say nothing of other possible side effects.

Will weightlifting stunt my growth?

No. There is no physiological basis for believing that weight training will shorten the height of an adolescent. There is some possibility that taking anabolic steroid drugs might, but good honest weight training will not.

Can I become muscle bound?

Yes and no. If you work out improperly by using a number of cheating exercises and by "pumping" the muscles with light weights, you may cause some loss of the full range of a limb's movement. Proper weight training may actually improve flexibility rather than hinder it. It is especially good to continue some form of stretching exercises during the weeks or months you train with weights. This will help your body get better accustomed to the added bulk you may acquire.

Which is better, barbells or weight machines?

The machines are safer and are easier to use because they do part of the work. How? Because the bars and handles on the various weight stations are attached to the machine, the muscular effort needed to balance the weight as well as lift it is not necessary. Less muscle fiber is placed under the stress.

A newer, more radical type of weight machine involving a cam to give heavy, even resistance throughout the range of exercise has not been thoroughly studied by the author. These pieces of equipment, referred to as nautilus machines, apparently give their users a very intense work-out in a short amount of time. These machines should not be used by teenagers without their first having very thorough training in their use and working out under close supervision.

Are some routines better than others?

Yes. You should only do those exercises that will best suit your needs. Do not do too many for one area of the body. Do not use some of the exercises which advanced bodybuilders or weightlifters use because you will receive very little benefit from them.

What are the best exercises?

Probably the bench press for the upper body and the squat for the lower body are the two best exercises. Both exercises work several muscles at a time. Much strength and quite a bit of muscular size can be added with just these two exercises.

Where can I get information about competing in a weightlifting or bodybuilding contest?

If you would like to enter a weightlifting contest, contact your local AAU official or check with the local YMCA about an AAU card and possible meets. An AAU membership card entitles you to compete in Amateur Athletic Union sanctioned contests. After you have your card and begin looking for a contest, remember that you have to be at least sixteen to enter a powerlifting meet. Many novice and teenage Olympic lifting meets are held throughout the nation but mostly in the Northeast and in California. However, most states usually have at least one novice (for beginners) or teenage meet a year.

If you desire to enter a bodybuilding contest, there are several things you should do to prepare yourself. First, make sure that you are built well-enough to enter without embarrassing yourself and your friends. Go see at least one physique contest before you enter one and see what kind of competition to expect. Second, practice a posing routine until you can go through a one-minute exhibition without thinking about your positions or movements from pose to pose. Be sure your poses show your build to its best advantage. Avoid poses that show any flaws in your physique. Do standard poses; there are many of them. Look poised and graceful as well as manly. Third, you will need to buy or have made a pair of posing trunks. These are about the size of swim trunks used in racing competition. They are brief but decent. Traditionally, bodybuilders shave the hair from their chest, back, arms, and legs in order that the muscular detail will show up more clearly. You do not have to do this, but you will certainly look out of place if all other contestants have done so.

Why should a naturally strong, quick, and coordinated athlete use weights?

Weight training can improve the performance of any athlete. Weight training can make the average athlete good and the good athlete excellent. Weight training will not work wonders, though. A boy who has poor coordination, below average flexibility, and is slow will not become the school's top quarterback or varsity wrestling champ even with the help of weights. He may, however, improve himself enough to make the team.

What sports does weight training help the most?

Of the major sports, wrestling and football show the best results.

Can any sport develop the muscle size and strength that weight training does?

No. Gymnasts and wrestlers probably come closest to having physiques which rival those of weightlifters.

Is there a best time of year to work out with weights?

For most people there is not. However, people who are overweight may find that heavy weight training in the summer will help them lose weight faster than it would in cooler months. The tendency to "sweat off" excess weight in the summer combined with the lighter appetites which some people have in the summertime could aid an obese person in losing extra pounds.

Why do most programs limit you to eight to ten repetitions for upper body exercises?

Generally, if a person can handle a weight properly for more than ten repetitions per set, he needs to use more weight. Doing high repetitions, say twenty, in doing curls "pumps" the muscle full of blood but does not seem to activate muscle tissue to actually grow as well as doing a lower number of repetitions and using a heavier weight.

What are "super sets"?

Super sets are combinations of exercises, usually two, sometimes more. The exercise combination is supposed to work the muscle harder and quicker to the point of fatigue. In super-setting, either two opposing muscles are worked or the same muscle is worked from an entirely different angle. The exercises are alternated without rest for the muscle. Super sets are performed by bodybuilders and advanced weight trainees who can handle the more rigorous pace. Two examples of super sets would be alternating curls and triceps extensions, or bench presses and the flying exercise.

How may weights be used for rehabilitation of a broken or damaged limb?

If you are recovering from a broken arm or knee operation, first, get your doctor's permission to use weights to rebuild the shrunken, weakened muscles. In fact, the doctor may suggest a rehabilitation program with weights for the affected area. Rebuilding an injured arm could start with the squeezing of a hard rubber ball to build up the grip, the wrist, and, to an extent, the forearm. From a hard rubber ball, one can then go to a spring hand grip or wrist rolls with a very light weight (2½ pounds or less). After further improvement in strength, regular curls and heavier wrist rolls can be done to get the arm back into top shape.

Getting over a knee injury or a broken leg bone requires time and patience. To rebuild and toughen muscles which have shrunk and weakened from lack of use, very light thigh extensions, leg presses, and/or thigh curls should be done in high repetitions. Increase the weight you are using about five pounds every week or so until the muscles are rebuilt.

How should I treat a muscle injury suffered during a workout?

First, let us establish one point—you will not injure any muscle in weight training unless you are doing something wrong. "Like what?" you may ask. Like not warming up properly, using a weight that is too heavy, or doing the exercise improperly. The most common muscle injury is a strained (or stretched) muscle. Sometimes light exercise actually seems to help a strained muscle; but generally, only rest, massage, cold treatments or heat will heal it. The same is true of a "pulled" muscle a situation where a muscle may be torn completely or partially from its connection to the bone. Whirlpool baths, therapeutic muscular massage, heating pads, hot water bottles, hot baths, and analgesic balms, as well as ice packs and icy whirlpools, all help restore strained or torn muscles to normal. However, giving the muscle a rest is best.

Will a girl become muscular like a boy if she uses weights?

No. Girls have a greater layer of fat underneath their skin. This gives a girl her softer, more rounded contours. Although a girl can become stronger through weight training as well as firm herself up, she is not going to develop the angular, muscular type physique of a male athlete. One basic biological difference between males and females is the greater abundance of hormones in the male which produce their large, defined muscles. So, although a girl can use weights to slim down and improve her strength, she will not develop a boy's muscularity.

Who is the strongest man of all time?

Many stories have come down through the years about the powerful feats of American and European men. Entire books have been written on strongman feats and stunts. Men like Louis Cyr, Herman Goerner, Eugene Sandow, and others performed many impressive feats during their lifetimes. They lifted weights, people, rocks, even cars, to show their great strength. In more modern times, Paul Anderson and the Russian heavyweight Vasily Alexeev would have to rank among the strongest men in the world. Anderson's six-thousand-pound backlift has never been excelled or even duplicated. Alexeev has clean and jerked over 550 pounds overhead—more than anyone else has ever done in competition.

Can I gain muscle and lose fat at the same time?

Yes, it's quite possible to use dieting and proper weight training to lose fat around the stomach, hips, and legs while increasing muscle size. The author has done this many times when going back into serious training. Unless you are grossly overweight, there should be no problem in growing firm muscle tissue while dieting and exercising fat away.

In what country is weightlifting the most popular?

There are more competitive lifters in Russia than in any other part of the world. Weightlifting is quite popular throughout most communist countries. Weightlifting champions in Russia and other communist states are looked upon as heroes. The Soviet Union gives its lifters good paying, easy jobs and even supplements their income.

Who is the world's best built man?

This is another tough question, and the answer lies pretty much in the eyes of the beholder. In the late 1930s, and through most of the 1940s, John Grimek was generally considered to be the best built man. Outstanding physiques proliferated in the fifties, but Reg Park of South Africa and Bill Pearl, Steve Reeves, Clancy Ross, and Jack Delinger in the United States were highly regarded. The 1960s saw the emergence of most of the great physiques that are still around today. Still highly regarded by most bodybuilding enthusiasts, Bill Pearl and Reg Park made it through the sixties. Larry Scott, Sergio Oliva, and Dave Draper were three top physique men of this period. Today's best known bodybuilder, Arnold Swarzenegger, began to win most of the major physique contests in the late sixties. At six feet two inches and two hundred forty pounds, with television show appearances and movie contracts, Swarzenegger is probably the best known bodybuilder in the world today. He is also probably the best built.

Are men who just work out for big muscles very strong?

That depends upon the man and his training program. Charles Estes of Tennessee, a good friend of the author, is also one of the top body-builders of the sixties. Although primarily a bodybuilder, Estes bench pressed 450 pounds in competition, and at one time did twenty-seven chins, while weighing 225 pounds. A bodybuilder may train with heavy weights and get extremely strong, or he may train with light to moderate weights and develop only mediocre strength.

Where can I learn the most about competitive weightlifting?

The York Barbell Club in York, Pennsylvania, has for years been considered the top weightlifting club in the United States. Making some trips to the York gym would be very advantageous to most serious lifters. The York team always has top lifters willing to give advice and help to newcomers.

How often should I change my workout?

If it's working, don't change your program for the sake of change. Change the routine when progress in gaining weight, size, and strength has stopped. You should evaluate your program for possible change once every twelve workouts. Drop exercises that do little good or at least change either the sets, repetitions, or weight you are using.

Is it all right to listen to music when you work out?

Sure, so long as it doesn't ruin your concentration. The right type of music might even help the training programs of some individuals who work out alone and dislike deathly silence. Don't bring your music to the gym when other members are present unless you know they don't mind.

Won't I increase my chance of getting ruptured by using heavy weights?

Ruptures or hernias have several causes, but weight training is rarely one of them. Many men who get hernias have inherited a weaker than average abdominal wall, and any undue strain as an adult can cause some part of the intestines to pop through the wall to the lower abdominal cavity. If you seriously abuse yourself while weight training by lifting weights improperly or lifting weights that are too heavy, then a hernia or rupture might possibly result. You would be much more likely, though, to suffer a torn muscle. Working out properly may actually strengthen the muscles of the abdomen enough to help prevent a rupture that might have taken place.

How do you know if you're above average in strength and muscularity?

You can tell by having lifting contests with friends and by comparing muscle measurements. The chapter "How to Know Your Own Strength" in this book should also help you. Be sure that you warm up properly for any contests that are held to test strength. One interesting strength statistic that has been around for years and still hasn't been proved or disproved is that only one boy or man in every one thousand can press his own weight without formal training on the press. Counting the adult population, this may be true; but among teenagers, several more than one out of a thousand can perform the stunt. A quick way to check your build is to measure your chest, waist, and hips. If the chest is seven inches or more larger than the waist measurement and three inches larger than the hips, you have a well-proportioned muscular build. Most adult males have a bigger hip than chest measurement.

Preventing the "Musclebound" Putdown

There are several things that the serious weight man can do to show that his hard-earned new muscles are just as flexible as the smaller ones he used to have. In fact, with a little extra work, the weight training enthusiast will be able to show greater flexibility than his buddies.

Let's take a look at flexibility. Some people are naturally more flexible than others. Younger children are more flexible than older children and adults.

Carl Betsch demonstrates the flexibility of a weight-trained athlete by touching his nose to the floor.

The term "double-jointed" is commonly used to describe people who can bend their thumbs back to their hands, sit down with their legs behind their backs, and do other almost "freakish" movements. This type of person is naturally gifted with greater muscle suppleness and looser bone-joint attachments than the average person. They really don't have double-joints.

At the other end of the picture we have the child or adult, even the athlete, who can't touch his fingers to his toes or scratch below the back of his neck.

Weight training on a regular basis can actually improve flexibility. By putting more stress on the muscle and moving it through a greater range of motions while doing a weight exercise, the muscle can easily be stretched to a greater extent than normal. Doing the exercise properly will prevent any overstretching or strain to the muscle and only a slight soreness will be felt. This soreness will diasppear as the muscle becomes accustomed to this new range of movement. One of the major reasons for always doing the exercises properly in weight training is that tightness is prevented and flexibility actually increased.

It should be stressed here again that the weightlifter should always spend a few minutes "loosening up" before attacking the weights. Exercises to stretch the shoulder girdle, trunk, hamstrings, and front thighs prior to the workout make even the "warm-up" sets go a little easier. Some stretching during and after the workout will add even more flexibility. Simple calisthenics such as alternating toe touches, trunk rotations, one and two-leg splits, and rotations of the shoulders and arms will provide that extra stretch.

So far, only flexibility of the muscle has been mentioned. What about the ability of a muscle to react to a signal from the brain in a smooth, fast manner—in other words, coordination? Physiologists have proven that a stronger muscle is a faster muscle. As long as an increase in size brings an increase in strength, a bigger muscle is a faster muscle. In other words, the muscles will consistently respond faster to your commands regardless of the activity if their strength has been increased.

Is this to say that a six foot, two-hundred pound bodybuilder who can bench press 450 pounds and has nineteen inch arms will defeat Jimmy Connors at tennis? No, of course not. Natural skill plus experience would prevent this. However, if there were two copies of Jimmy Connors and one was to develop the physical size and capabilities mentioned above, while retaining the same skill and expertise, he would be the winner.

Take a look at the way athletes who depend upon extremely quick reflexes and split-second timing are built. Look at gymnasts and at acrobats. Their strong, above average size muscles are built from the demanding training they do. Yet, the superb coordination of these athletes cannot be doubted.

Professional football players, college basketball stars, Olympic caliber swimmers, and major league baseball players all use weight training to get the increased muscle speed, the faster reaction time, and the quicker recovery that comes from great strength.

HOW TO WIN OVER DOUBTERS

Showing that flexibility hasn't been swapped for bigger muscles is easy. Show off your flexibility with these simple feats:

Practice touching the toes, stretching a little more each time. Work to a point where the palms of the hands can be placed and held flat against the floor.

Work gradually toward a double split until your buttocks touch the floor. Work on splitting out just one leg at a time until you can touch it. Then work with the other leg until a full split can be done anytime. (Make sure that the pants or jeans will hold up before doing one.)

The split should be done before, during, and after workouts to stretch the muscles and maximize flexibility. Here, Carl Betsch is in the near low position.

Sit down with the legs stretched out to each side. Practice bending at the waist while holding on to the toes. When the waist can be bent enough to touch the nose to the floor, excellent flexibility is just around the corner.

Some of the qualities of a well-coordinated person can't be shown except in competition, whether it be team play, one-on-one, or with the use of special equipment. However, there are several tried and true feats of coordination where the stronger man has the advantage:

Carl Betsch is here captured right at the "clap" of the Marine push-up. This quite remarkable photo was taken at 1/1000 of a second.

Marine Push-Up

The so-called Marine Push-Up combines strength and good timing. Practice a strong push from the floor that will take the torso higher than the regular push-up. As the chest reaches its high point off the ground, quickly bring your arms up and under your chest, clapping the hands together. Right before your body hits the floor, return your hands to their positions on the floor. This clap of the hands must be done very quickly. Big muscles don't go well with a flat nose.

A   B   C

D   E

Four stages to headstand, a matter of coordination and balance for student Carl Scarbrough who obliged us by turning to face front.

Headstand

Get into a squatting position with the arms placed between the legs and the hands placed slightly in front of the knees. Change weight of the body from the legs to the arms by uncurling the legs behind you while moving the head and torso forward of your hands. Place the top of the head on the ground and kick up the legs. After a few tries, you should be doing a headstand. From the headstand try pushing off into a handstand and holding it.

Walking Handstand

Place the arms out in front of the body. Kick up with the legs. Shift the weight to your hands and hold the legs straight up or bent at the knee. Walk about on the hands to maintain balance. Practice until it is possible to walk either forward or backward several feet.

Carl Betsch takes a quick "stroll" on the Hixson High campus.

A physical education teacher or gymnastics instructor may be able to suggest other feats of flexibility and good coordination that take strength to perform properly.

How to Know Your Own Strength

There are a number of ways the weight training student or weightlifter can tell if he is strong. The tests that follow apply regardless of whether the individual is thirteen or eighteen when compared to the average adolescent. However, in the case of good all-around athletes, the percentage of teenagers capable of these feats will increase with physical maturity.

You are strong if:

- You can press your body weight without having ever used weights. This is very difficult without some weight training.

- You can press your body weight after some weight training. No cheating, no clean-and-jerk, no "jumping it up."

- You can curl seventy-five percent of your body weight eight times strictly.

- You can curl your body weight once.

- You can do fifty push-ups straight anytime you choose.

- You can do at least ten strict chins.

- You can do fifteen dips on the parallel bars.

- You can bench press your own body weight ten times.

- You can bench press one and a half times your body weight once.

- You can press another person over your head who weighs seventy-five percent of your weight.

- You can beat over half of the people you arm wrestle.

- You can do ten full-squats with one and a half times your body weight.

- You can do ten handstand push-ups against a wall.

- You can walk on your hands for ten seconds.

- You can do ten push-ups with someone on your back who weighs at least seventy-five percent of your weight.

Fifty Weight Training Dos and Don'ts

1. *Do* read or follow instructions carefully before doing a new exercise.
2. *Don't* make the mistake of many beginners in doing exercises incorrectly.
3. *Do* dress properly for a workout. Wear sweats in winter or gym shorts and T-shirt in summer. Always wear shoes.
4. *Don't* leave your body uncovered, especially the torso. Keeping the muscles warm reduces the chance of injury.
5. *Do* ask your doctor if it's okay to work out.
6. *Don't* work out when heart and respiratory problems are present unless the doctor says okay.
7. *Do* get a training partner or two, if possible.
8. *Don't* do heavy bench presses or squats without a spotter; that is, a helper.
9. *Do* give a new training program a chance. Stay with it for nine workouts or longer.
10. *Don't* change exercises after a few workouts.
11. *Don't* get in a habit of cheating on the exercises.
12. *Do* everything as strictly as possible for maximum gains.
13. *Do* lighten your workout load when taking part in a sports program. Reduce the number of exercises.
14. *Don't* quit working out completely. Weekends are a good time to do some in-season training.
15. *Do* adjust your training program according to the time and energy you have left after practice.
16. *Do* try a circuit training program if you plan to play a sport that involves more endurance than explosive power.
17. *Don't* skimp on sleep.
18. *Do* get eight to ten hours of sleep each night.
19. *Do* get plenty of proteins, vitamins, and other nutrients.
20. *Don't* be misled into wasting money on needless vitamins and protein.
21. *Do* take vitamin and protein supplements if the regular meals don't yield enough.
22. *Do not* try to use an advanced person's weight poundage and program without adjusting them to your ability.
23. *Do* seek good advice about weights from more knowledgeable individuals.

24. *Do* follow closely the training advice in this book.
25. *Do not* send away for mail-order muscle-building gimmicks.
26. *Do* remember that weight training builds stronger and larger muscles faster than any other method.
27. *Do not* take anabolic steroid drugs.
28. *Do* tell friends about the possible harmful side effects steroid drugs may have.
29. *Do not* train without someone within shouting distance if working out alone.
30. *Do* tell someone that you are planning to work out if you plan to work out alone.
31. *Do* measure your progress with a reliable tape measure every twelve to fifteen workouts.
32. *Don't* measure yourself. Let someone more objective do it.
33. *Do not* be disappointed with small gains. A one-fourth or one-half inch gain in size can make a visible difference.
34. *Do not* work out every day unless you are on a split routine or are trying to lose weight.
35. *Do* work out regularly three times a week or every other day.
36. *Do* shower after a workout with warm water and soap to wash away bacteria and increase blood circulation through the muscles.
37. *Do not* shower and then go out into the cold air without properly drying first, especially your hair.
38. *Do not* show off in the weight room.
39. *Do* discourage others from trying lifts that might result in injury.
40. *Do* buy copies of weightlifting and bodybuilding journals for information and inspiration.
41. *Don't* try to use training programs in magazines that are too advanced or require equipment you don't have.
42. *Do not* buy equipment if it can be made or borrowed.
43. *Do* buy good quality weights and exercise equipment.
44. *Do not* work out under the influence of alcoholic beverages, marijuana, or other drugs. That is courting disaster.
45. *Do* work out before eating a meal, or wait an hour after eating.
46. *Do not* work out with weights that are too light.
47. *Do* work out with enough weight to build lasting muscles and greater strength.
48. *Do not* overbuild one or two parts of the body. Strive for a balanced, pleasing build.
49. *Do* have your friends buy this book.
50. *Don't* loan them your copy.

Nutrition

At any age, eating the proper foods is very important. For boys between thirteen and eighteen who use weights, getting the proper nutrition from foods is especially important.

Although you probably learned something about nutrition in your science or health classes, this review includes the merits of necessary vitamins and minerals as they relate to weight training. So here, again, are the essential vitamins: what foods contain them, and why the body needs them.

VITAMIN A

This vitamin is needed for good night vision or seeing any time light is limited. It is also necessary for normal tissue growth. Vitamin A aids in keeping moist tissues healthy, particularly the passages of the nose and throat. An overdose of vitamin A is possible, however. It should not be taken in large quantities, especially over an extended period. Vitamin A poisoning may cause malformation of the bone structure in young children and has other undesirable side effects for adults.

Sources of vitamin A include dairy products, dark green vegetables, and liver, the best source.

VITAMIN C

Highly useful, this vitamin is also highly controversial. Vitamin C definitely helps to heal wounds, prevent infection, form bones and teeth properly, and strengthen body tissues. Some scientists, many health food advocates and millions of ordinary citizens are convinced that vitamin C helps to prevent and cure the common cold. Some scientists who deny this say the vitamin will only lessen the common cold's symptoms.

There is also an unfounded belief among some bodybuilders, other athletes and fitness advocates that above average amounts of vitamin C will help prevent soreness. They believe it helps the body's muscle cells rid themselves of the toxic waste brought on by vigorous exercise. Sources of vitamin C include fresh citrus fruit, peppers, raw cabbage, melons, tomatoes, and turnip greens.

VITAMIN D

This vitamin is a must for strong bones and teeth. It helps the body to properly use calcium and phosphorous—two elements necessary for proper skeletal growth. Lack of this vitamin can cause various bone and spinal deformities. Vitamin D is usually added to milk, probably the chief source for most people. It is also found in small amounts in such foods as liver, egg yolk, and butter. Better sources of vitamin D are fish, particularly sardines, salmon, and tuna. Some vitamin D is obtained from sunlight. Not that sunlight itself contains the vitamin, but it does cause a chemical reaction in your body which produces the vitamin.

VITAMIN E

This vitamin prevents certain natural oxidations, the breaking down of body tissues, from getting out of hand and damaging these same tissues. Many nonscientific people make great claims for vitamin E's effects in preventing certain diseases, increasing longevity (the length of time that you live), and increasing sexual potency. Many athletes and physical fitness enthusiasts believe that vitamin E increases endurance. Sources for this vitamin include whole grains, wheat germ, meat, eggs, liver, butter, margarine, and leafy vegetables.

VITAMIN K

This vitamin is necessary for the liver to function correctly and it also aids in the proper clotting of blood. Vitamin K is found in eggs, liver, green leafy vegetables, alfalfa, and cauliflower.

MINERALS

To achieve the maximum from weight training, it is also a good idea to have an adequate supply of various minerals necessary for the body. These include iron, calcium, phosphorous, magnesium, iodine, fluoride, sodium, potassium, and trace amounts of some other elements.

PROTEIN

Since protein is the most essential nutrient in building larger and stronger muscle tissue, protein-rich foods should be high on the list of any weight trainer's diet. Protein can be obtained from animal or vegetable sources. Meat protein is usually of greater biological value than vegetable protein. That is, the body is able to use a greater percentage of the animal protein ingested. The established minimum daily requirement of protein for the adult is sixty grams. Active young people need more, particularly if those young people are working with weights to become larger and stronger. One hundred to one hundred-fifty grams per day should be the protein goal of weight training students. Animal protein can be obtained from beef, liver, poultry, fish, eggs, and milk. Good sources of vegetable protein include soybeans and peanuts. Following is a more complete listing of various foods and their protein content.

Protein Chart

Adapted from U.S. Government *Agriculture Handbook Number 8*

FOODS	PROTEIN*
Almonds, dried	18.6
Bacon, Canadian	20.0
Beans, white and cooked	7.8
Beef, raw (good grade)	18.5
Beef, raw (hamburger)	17.9
Beef, raw (choice grade)	17.4
Bologna, all meat	13.3
Bran, added sugar and malt extract	12.6
Brazil nuts	14.3
Bread, cracked wheat	8.7
Bread, white and enriched	8.7 to 9.0
Bread, white and unenriched	8.7 to 9.0
Bread, whole wheat	10.5
Buckwheat, whole grain	11.7
Buttermilk, from skim milk	3.6
Chocolate, candy with peanuts	14.1
Cheese, cottage	13.6
Cheese, natural and cheddar	25.0
Cheese, pasteurized American	23.2
Cheese, pasteurized Swiss	26.2
Cheese, Swiss (domestic)	27.5
Chicken, dark	20.6
Chicken, white	23.4
Chick-peas	20.5
Cod, cooked	28.5
Cornmeal, whole ground	9.2
Eggs, raw	12.9
Flounder, cooked	30.0
Frankfurters, all meat	13.1
Gelatin dessert, plain	1.5
Halibut, cooked	25.2
Lamb, raw (choice grade)	16.5
Liver, beef and raw	19.9
Liver, chicken and raw	19.7
Liver, hog and raw	20.6
Macaroni, dry enriched	12.5
Mackerel, raw	19.0
Milk, cow (3.7 percent fat)	3.5
Milk, cow (2.0 percent non-fat solids added)	4.2
Milk, cow (dry non-fat powder)	35.8
Oatmeal, cooked	2.0
Oats, rolled dry	14.2

*Amount of protein is grams per 3.5 ounces (100 grams) food.

Food	Protein*
Ocean perch, raw	19.0
Peanut butter, added fat and salt	27.8
Peanut butter, sweetened	25.2
Peanuts, roasted and salted	26.0
Peanuts, roasted with skins	26.2
Perch, yellow raw	19.5
Pork, raw and total edible:	
(medium fat)	15.7
(thin class)	16.7
Pumpkin seed kernels	29.0
Rice, brown and raw	7.5
Rye, flours and medium	11.4
Rye, flours and dark	16.3
Rye, whole grain	12.1
Safflower seed, kernels and dry	19.1
Salami, cooked	17.5
Salmon, solids (Pink and canned)	20.5
Salmon, solids (Sockeye and canned)	20.3
Soybeans, mature seeds and raw	34.1
Soybeans, mature seeds and cooked	11.0
Soybean flours, high fat	41.2
Soybean flours, low fat	43.2
Soybean protein	74.9
Spaghetti, dry and enriched	12.5
Sunflower seeds, flour and defatted	45.2
Sunflower seeds, kernels dry	24.0
Tuna	24.2
Turkey, raw and edible	20.1
Veal, raw and medium fat	12.4
Wheat, bran	16.0
Wheat, cereal (ready-to-eat flakes)	10.2
Wheat flour, all purpose and enriched	10.5
Wheat, germ	20.6
Wheat, puffed	15.0
Wheat, wheat germ cereal	20.2
Yeast (brewer's)	38.8

*Amount of protein is grams per 3.5 ounces (100 grams) food.

Weight Training and Your Lifestyle

Weight training journals have printed countless stories over the years of how using weights has dramatically changed someone's life for the better. Some of these stories are probably true, many may be exaggerated, but many real life accounts of the beneficial effects of weights do exist. This author has met several successful businessmen who swear that the confidence and self-esteem they gained through weight training enabled them to rise to the top of their professions. Teachers have remarked to parents on the transformation of youngsters from insecure to confident, only to learn that the boys had taken up weight training. Working out with weights gives one a chance to meet friends with mutual interests. Weight training can turn a few hours a week of wasted time into a very constructive, self-bettering, healthful time.

Recently a friend of the author's was involved in an auto accident. His four-wheel drive vehicle turned over on its top and was totaled. The doctors said that the heavy musculature of this former top-ranked bodybuilder acted as a cushion—a veritable wall of shock absorbers that saved his life. They said a normal person would have died in the wreck.

How useful is weight-trained muscle? To a business person or homemaker, the extra strength and muscle tone will allow household and yard chores to be done with less strain, effort, and fatigue.

Weight-trained muscles are better than non-weight-trained muscles, all other factors being equal. A 160-pound athlete with little off-season conditioning will usually come out second best to the same athlete who is strong and quick and in shape thanks to weight training.

There are some types of movements in wrestling or motions in football and other sports where superior strength matters very little. A strong athlete may have no advantage over a weaker one in certain situations. In fact, a skilled wrestler can often use his opponent's superior strength to beat him if that wrestler tries to "out-muscle" his opponent to win. However, in many situations throughout the sports world, greater strength will win out every time.

A successful weight training enthusiast should try to present a good image for weight training. Don't become one of those types who can't pass a mirror without flexing an arm or throwing out the chest. Such acts of narcissism or self-love result in ridicule instead of respect from friends and strangers alike.

Never make weight training an all-consuming passion. Sure, you must train hard and train often to be a successful bodybuilder or competitive lifter, but this should only be one aspect of a well-rounded life. Weight training should add a new dimension to one's lifestyle, not make it one-sided. As nice as seventeen-inch arms and four-hundred-pound bench presses are, these achievements should be looked at in the context of the whole person and not be singular, one track goals. The obligations that you have to your family, church, school, and friends should never suffer because of weight training. Have the best of both worlds. Use the new-found strength and confidence of weight training to create in yourself a more complete person.

David Salstrand defeats an opponent during the '76-'77 wrestling season.

Index